M C B A G

Marin County Bad Art Gallery

Celebrating Creative Failure

Marin County Bad Art Gallery MCBAG
Celebrating Creative Failure

MCBAG is intended as entertainment, satirizing and speculating on the motives and materials that might have been sourced in creating the artwork included in this collection.

No product, company, or person mentioned in this book has endorsed, authorized, or sponsored this book. We don't wish to compete in any way, or cause any confusion, so we want to be clear - any references to these (and any other) brand names and or trademarks are made in parody of imagined artists' materials, or critics' highfalutin art-speak:

Jolly Rancher™, Dentyne® gum, Hefty® bags, Starbucks frappuccino®, Cool Whip™, Rabbit™, PETA®, McDonalds®, Coors®, The Oakland Raiders™, Olde English 800®, Masonite™, KFC®, Cards Against Humanity™, Testors® glue, Brawny® paper towels, Gatorade®, Mütter Museum™, My Little Pony®, Nutella®, Peeps®, Ziplock® bags, Pilot® pens, Vicks® Nyquil™, and Fredericks of Hollywood™. The brand names and trademarks mentioned are not used seriously, but only in jest.

If anyone has new, or possibly different information about any of the artists or the paintings (or the artistic mediums employed) in MCBAG, please contact us so that we can correct any errors in the next edition.

- Dedication -

To the muse - may she never forget where we live, and always find an open door when she comes to call.

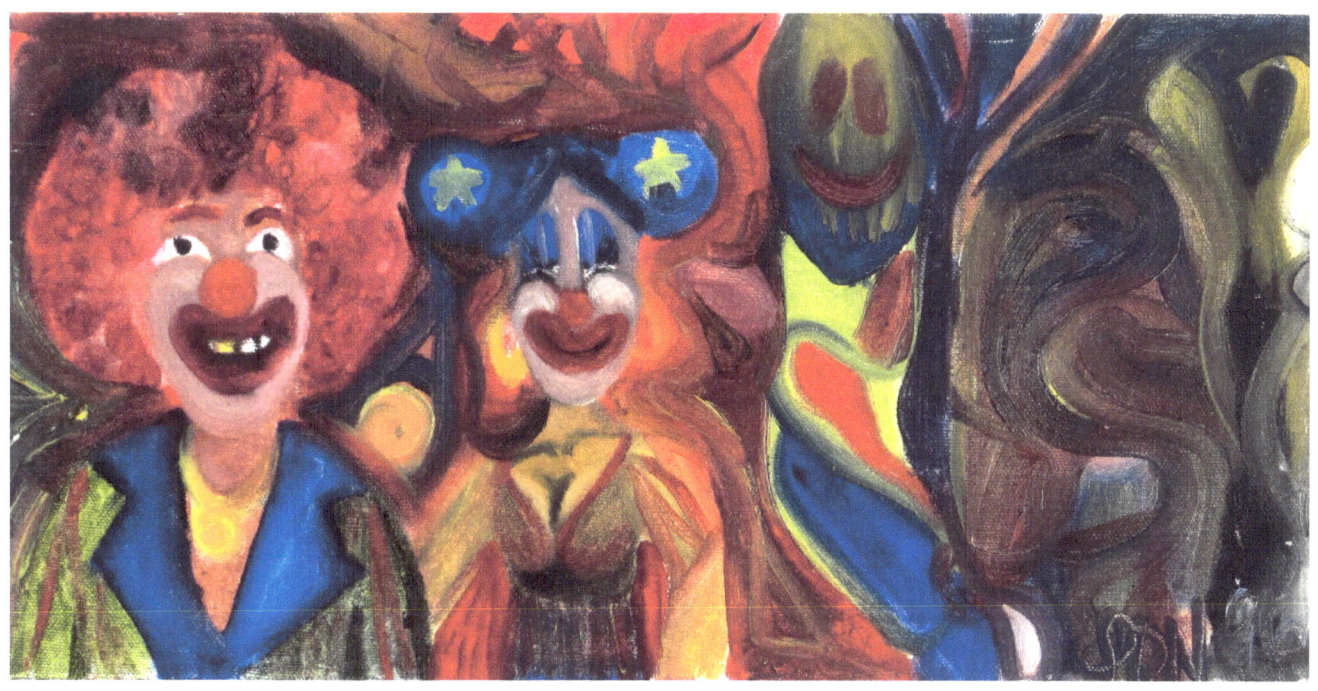

"Everyone Loves a Clown"
Prunella D.Naka, 1996
Acrylic on Canvas

"The child's laughter is pure until he first laughs at a clown."

- Angela Carter, author

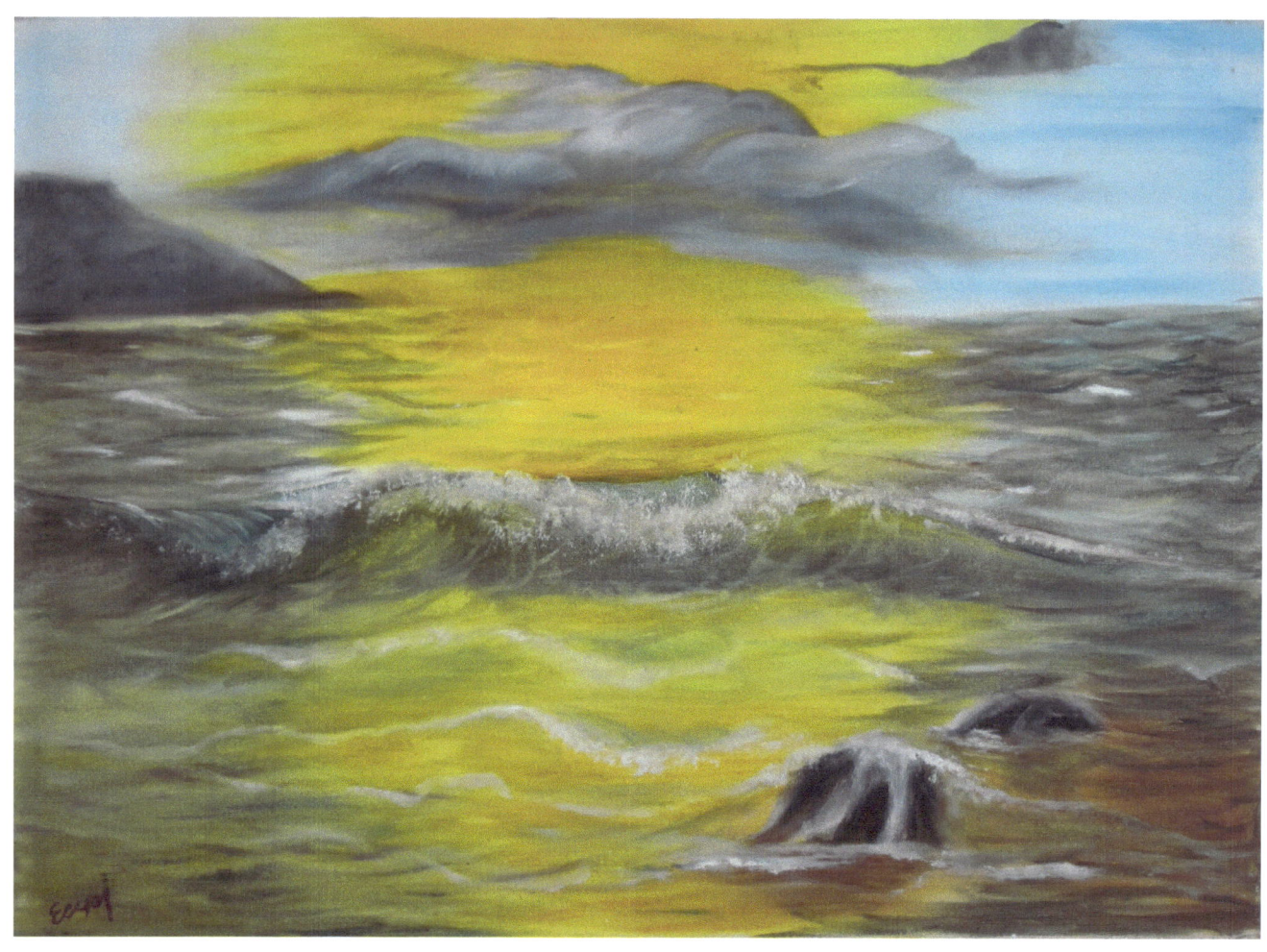

"The Ninth Wave Revisited"
Ecyoj (Joyce spelled backwards), 1999
Oil on canvas

Inspired by 19th century masters of water art like Ivan Aivazovsky and Anders Zorn, Ecyoj felt moved to convey her great affection for the eternal beauty of ocean waves. The inspiration came during a hearty breakfast of undercooked huevos rancheros with no toast to wipe the plate clean. The potent yellow and red hues that dominate the piece and distract the viewer from any other potentially redeeming feature are symbolic of the runny yolk and hot salsa, respectively. One is forced to ponder: why were the eggs so undercooked? Who prepared such a haphazard meal? Why not simply scramble the eggs? Since its release, the work has held a contentious place in the art historian community sparking vitriolic disagreement between two camps that have formed: those that prefer their eggs poached and those that prefer over easy. The unforeseen impact of this masterpiece has left the world eagerly anticipating the artist's next release.

A.O.

"An empty canvas is a living wonder… far lovelier than certain pictures."

- Wassily Kandinsky

INTRODUCTION

The book in your hands is a collection of what we at MCBAG (Marin County Bad Art Gallery) consider to be "bad art". They are by and large, lovable freaks, irregulars, defects and oddities that we have deemed worthy of saving from thrift stores, trashcans, dark dank basements, sidewalk freebees and yard sales. Patiently we have gathered them together, assigned accession numbers to each one, written wall text for them and put them on a website, mcbagcollection.com. Now, at the urging of many of our friends and going against all of our left leaning philosophical values, we have decided to brazenly monetize the concept.

Many times we have been asked how we got started in collecting "bad art". Upon reflection, we realized our interest, albeit in a different form, began long ago. For decades we had enjoyed laughing at comedians like Buster Keaton, Charlie Chaplin, Laurel and Hardy and Woody Allen. The movie "Gizmo", the TV show *In Living Color*, and the absolutely brilliant *Mystery Science Theatre 3000* have also given us hours of nonstop laughter. The single most endearing quality that attracted us to them was their ability to find humor in human failure. At MCBAG we celebrate *creative* failure; understanding that it is much better to laugh and try again than to cry and give up. More broadly, the quotes from the masters that can be seen on many of the following pages demonstrate how important the role of failure is in the process of learning and the development of tremendous talent and genius.

A few folks have been critical of our project, claiming that we should not laugh at the creative efforts of other people and this can only have a demoralizing effect on artists. While we thank them for expressing their opinions, we would reply: In an era of "A" average, "everybody gets a ribbon", and classroom "critiques" in name only, our opinions are somewhat different. On the long road to mastering any skill, there are stages of development; they should be recognized, honored and considered not only with respect to our own work, but also in relation to all the masters that have come before us. How many of us while in art school have been so proud of our student "masterpieces", only to look at them a year later and find them cringe worthy? In light of this, we suggest that we take the *process* of learning seriously, but not so much the *products* of learning. We encourage students (and we are all students, really) to relax, enjoy the experience and have some fun along the way.

In our frequent trips to art galleries and museums we have often felt frustrated, annoyed or amused at the highbrow way in which the wall texts that accompany the artworks are written. While we have great respect for the art authorities' years of training, education, and experience, at MCBAG we occasionally poke some well-meaning fun at their "art speak". We hope that they will forgive our parody and receive it in the lighthearted spirit that it is meant.

These topics raise some serious questions: Why do we make art? What purpose, if any, does it serve in our lives? Can elephants really paint? Is Cristo a *real* artist or just an environment-trashing egotist? Wrecking marriages, dinner parties, bank accounts and self-esteem, these and many other issues are hotly debated in the hallowed halls of the Creative Ones. And *until* the art polemics are resolved, we at MCBAG will remain ever-vigilant thrift store bottom feeders and bad art impresarios extraordinaire applying great unyielding truths enhanced by the time honored tickle system.

So, grab a glass of wine, sit back and have some fun with this visual offering!

The MCBAG Overlords - November 2016

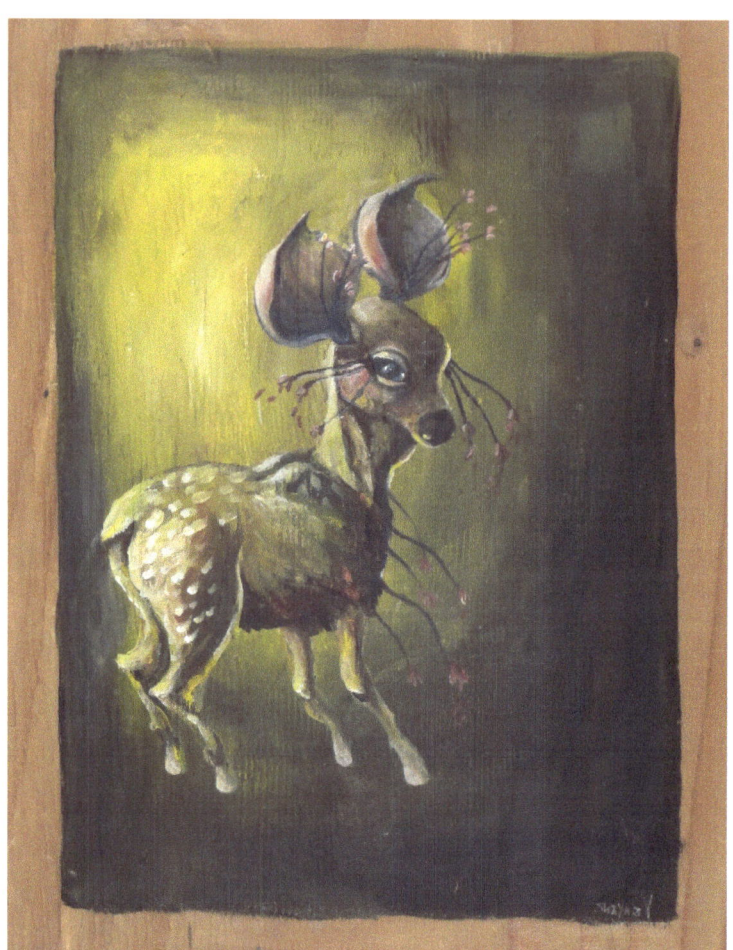

"The Artist As Main Course"
Luvart Gotscrewd, 1975
Oil on plywood

Here is an innocent fawn; so vulnerable it still has its protective spotted camouflage. One day it is gamboling about enjoying its sylvan freedom and the next it is covered with flesh eating fiends, dripping blood while they parasitize its orifices. In this nightmarish painting, our artist is consumed by the professional art gallery world. They attempt to digest him completely from the inside out as they assault the twin high alters of creativity, his heart and brain. Staggering toward the dingy yellow light of wrecked hope in the distance, the little deer glances back with painful resignation, warning all artists they are forever doomed within this profit driven machine. Viewed backwards in a mirror, his rump spots spell the word Banksy.

K.L.

"Love on the Rocks / Another Night on the Couch"
Fatbardh Fisnik, 1962
Graphite, India ink on paper

Barbie's been hitting the sauce again - experimenting this time with her special concoction of Vicks Nyquil, ayahuasca and vodka. Just for Ken she is wearing her new Fredericks of Hollywood bra. The hallucinations are well underway as the world's biggest transistor radio blasts out Jim Morrison's "Light My Fire". The music flows across the floor and slides up the walls. A spilled ink blob, like an ethereal specter, floats up in the corner waiting to smother any unsuspecting victim. Arriving home after a long day at the office Ken pauses, realizing he won't be having his sex change talk with her tonight.

K.L.

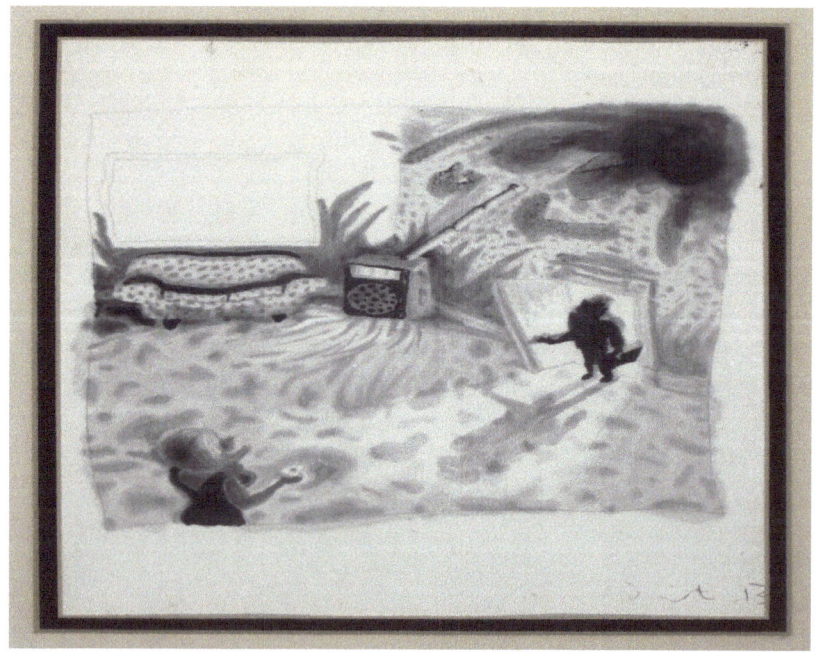

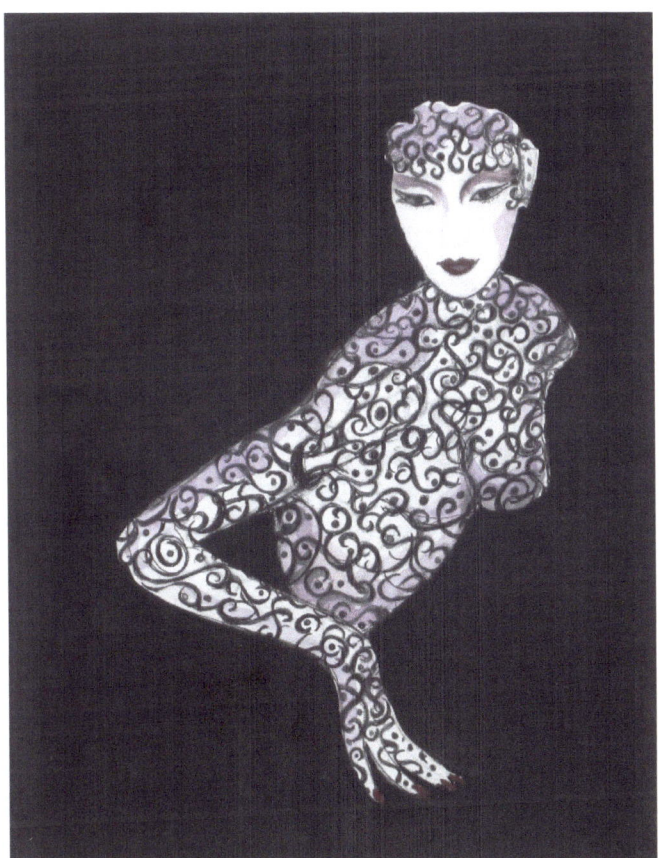

"Lady Longevin"
Annie Hart, 2008
Watercolor and graphite on paper

Talented Sonoma County artist Annie Hart has created, through the skillful use of negative space and flawless composition, this intriguing portrait of her grandmother. Hart has captured the mysterious feline quality of Lady Longevin, who was a famous depression era actress and circus sideshow performer. Known for her role in the 1932 pre code movie "Freaks" this beautiful hemimorph stole the show every time she hopped onto the set. When not acting, she packed in audiences at Barnum and Bailey's circus where crowds thrilled to see her breath taking flying trapeze triple spins. To explain the origin of her curiously cranium-less head, the star revealed that it was the result of a high wire training accident at the beginning of her career. "Y'know, you got to work with what ya have, so I just got tatted up and kept on goin'," she replied. Upon her passing, the artist donated her grandmother's remains to Philadelphia's Mutter Museum where it floats in a 20-gallon formaldehyde pickle jar.

K.L.

"Vision is the art of seeing what is invisible to others."
- Jonathan Swift

"It is the Only Way / Thorn 1"
General Galantinissimo Gilmour, 2015
A slurry of subsurface silica, red hiparrion ash and repurposed manteca on canvas

We must all consent to become one of the people, worship the creator, and agree to the insertion of the instrument of obedience. Resistance is futile.

K.L.

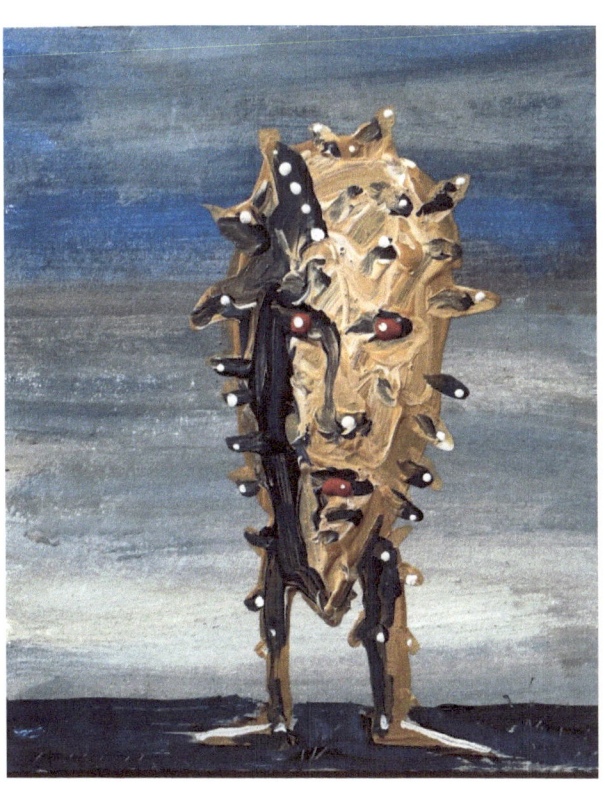

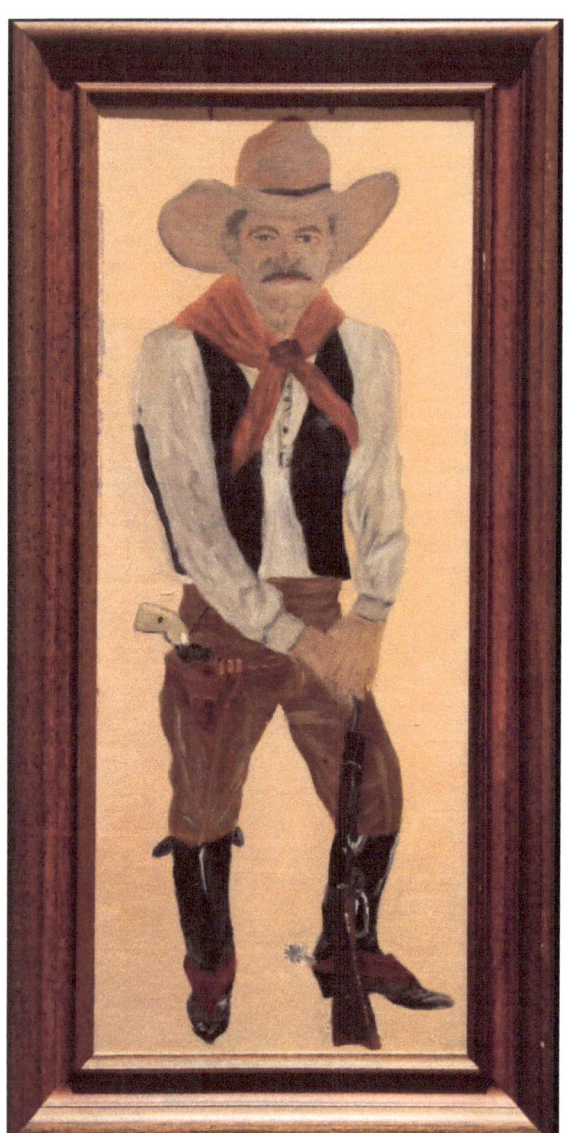

"Ready For Action"
Squirrel Tooth Alice, 1886
Oil on stretched cowhide

In 1886 Squirrel Tooth Alice, infamous madam of Dodge City, Kansas, painted this portrait of her equally famous gunslinger, outlaw boyfriend Waddy Peacock Knudsen. As a contemporary of Frederick Remington, she was well known throughout the West for her portraits of the men she had entertained at her establishment. She claimed she liked the little "knuckle draggin' guys" because, "the ones with the short legs were always so polite and grateful. And they compensated for their little legs in other ways," she stated matter-of-factly. Alice has carefully composed this painting so that the viewer's eye travels from Waddy's arrestingly hungry gaze to his highly polished pearl handled gun. Barely contained by its holster it juts out suggestively from the lawman's hip. It is said that this painting was finished just moments before Knudsen, in a moment of carelessness, blew off his left arm with an unfortunate shotgun blast.

K.L.

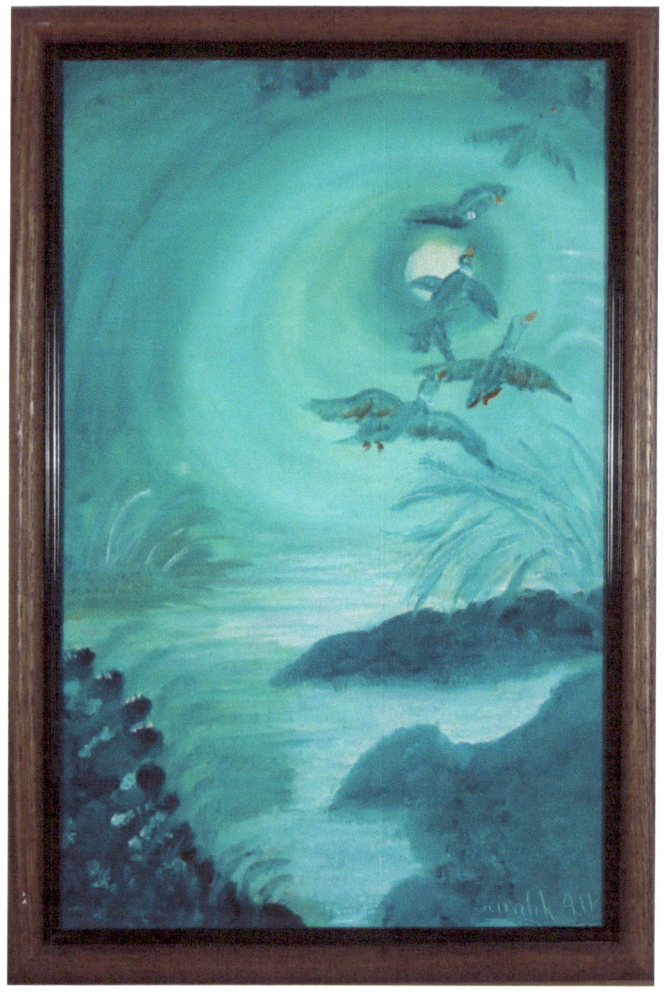

"Yucatan Hellhole / Seamus O'Mallard"
Sarah K. Allen, 1962
Acrylic on canvas

We keep trying really hard to like this painting. After all, it has a tragically dying green stegosaurus (lower left) and 5 (6?) pretty little green ducks attempting desperately to fly through the thick green air over a green hazy swamp past an indistinct green jungle. But let's face it. This is a monochromatic mess with a vaguely post apocalyptic, day-after-the-meteorite-hit the Yucatán, feeling about it; Allen could have at least put a rescue jet ski in the misty distance, or a Precambrian mammal with little grasping flippers hanging onto a rock to give us a shred of hope for our distant future.

K.L.

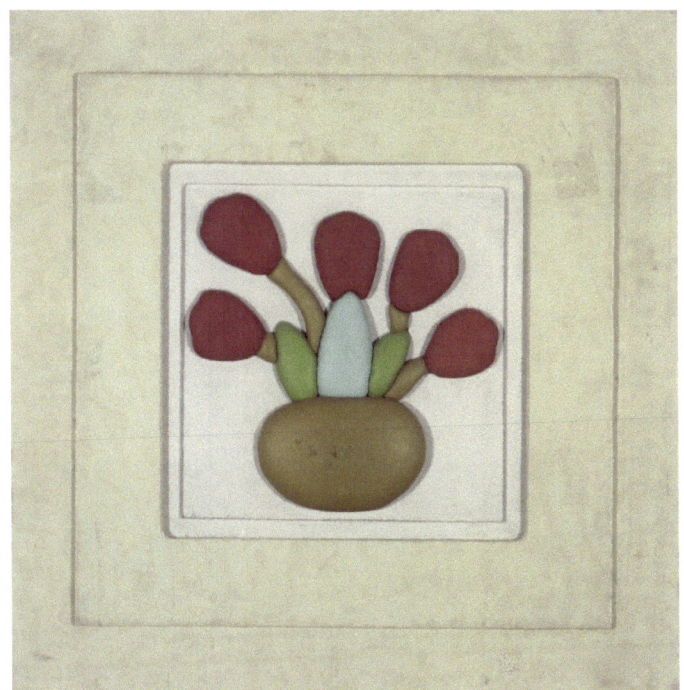

"Red Swollen Rosettes In a Vase-Like Thing"
Gimolina Grandeflora, 1983
Minature Nauga hides, fluffy stuff and cardboard

As creative guru and lead artist at the School of Hospitality Arts and Hotel Arrangements (SOHAHA) Grandeflora has created hundreds of the finest innocuous motel room wall decorations (we just can't call them art) in an effort to enhance the guests' viewing pleasure. We find them remarkable in their complete unremarkableness. It is rumored that Grandeflora, having finally tapped out her talent in that field, moved on to design washable assless chaps, movement activated bull whips and a variety of fetish wear.

K.L.

"We have art in order not to die of the truth."
- Friedrich Nietzsche

"Chernobyl Wine Country"
Matvei Belsky, 2010
Some sort of glowing paints on canvas

Sign up now for a carefree, 2 week tour and nothing but fun in the Ukrainian sun! After just one day of sampling delicious Cabernets in this trendy new vacation hot spot, you will become your own nightlight!

K.L.

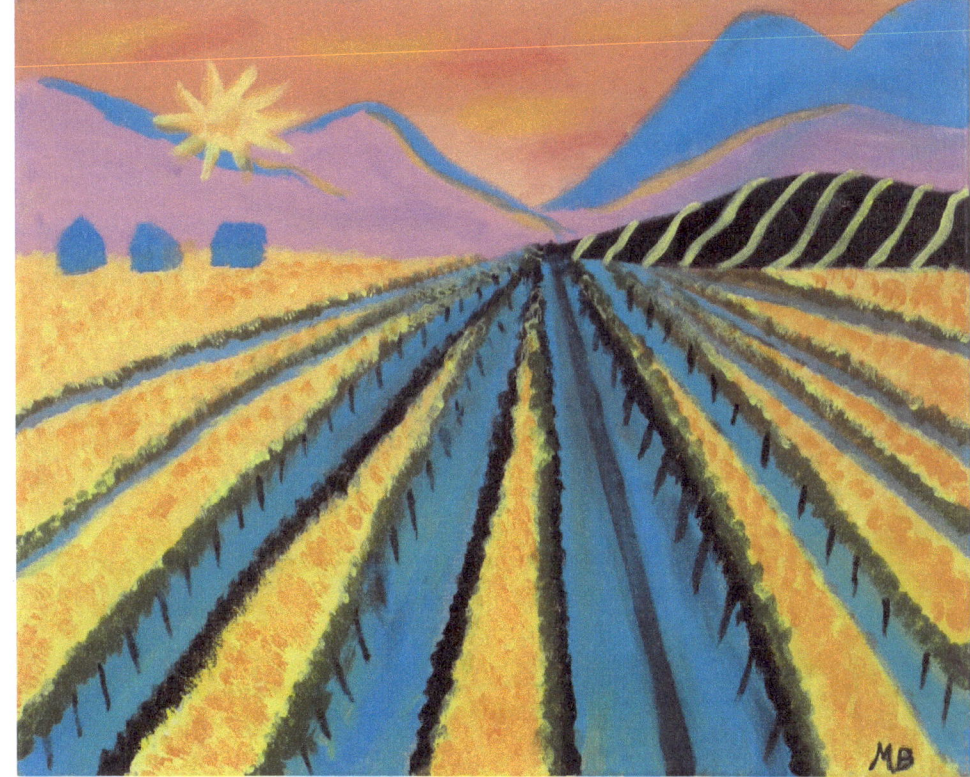

9

"Wake Up, Eat, Poop, Sleep, Repeat"
Artist Unknown, 1994 give or take 10 years
Acrylic on canvas

Groggy from a 17 hour nap Mr. Spunky awakes and contemplates his most important life challenges: should he lick his tail, lick his testicles or taste some of the clove studded Christmas ham he lays on? Through the miserly use of paints and the enthusiastic emphasis on clove dots, our unknown artist has masterfully captured the everyday dilemmas that face America's aging tomcats while causing us to long for glazed yams. You know - the kind with toasted marshmallows, all puffy on top.

K.L.

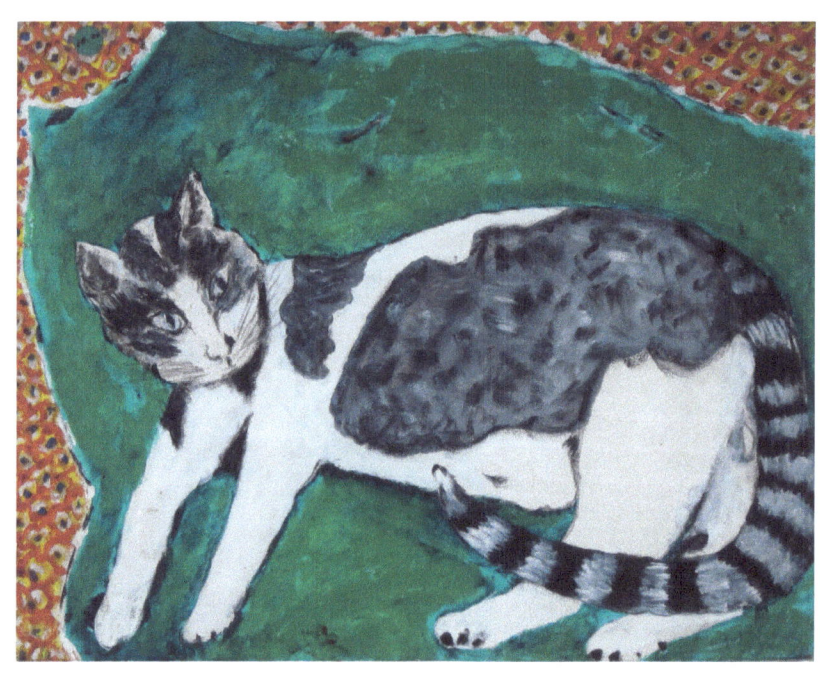

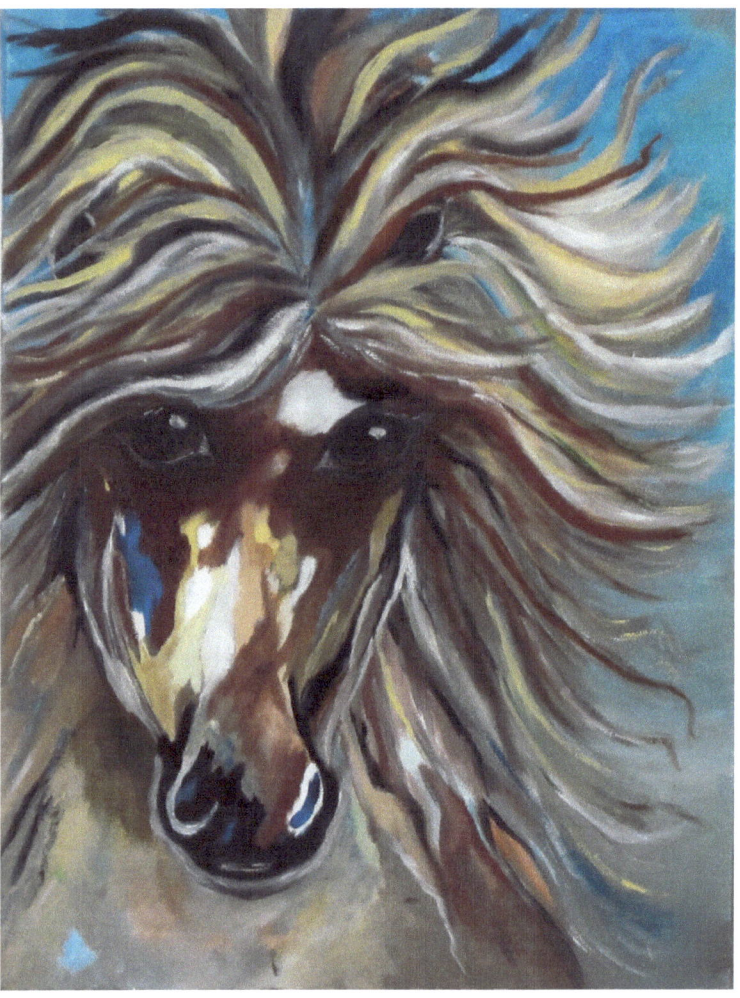

"I've failed again!"
- Vincent Van Gogh

"Hairy Creature With Brown Eyes"
Clancy Carson, 2005
Acrylic on canvas

Carson studied for years at the Margaret Keane School of portraiture before venturing out on her own. In her first solo offering, she has created what seems to be a genetic experiment that combines the best qualities of Farrah Fawcett, My Little Pony and Aatifa the Afghan hound. Its human like eyes beg us for some cream rinse.

K.L.

"Glory to God in the Highest Forever (Dio Nel piu Alto dei Cieli)"
Nonna Maria Delizioso, 2005
Velveeta Cheese product, marshmallow cream, and Dentyne gum on canvas

Before she passed away in 2005 Nonna Delizioso made one last attempt to express her devotion to God and Velveeta cheese product at once in this supremely tactile work of simplistic adoring beauty. Her faithfully meticulous daubing of a unique secret mixture of Dentyne gum and Marshmallow cream creates a dreamy effect as if a disembodied godhead were floating thru the aftermath of an explosion in a goose down pillow factory. By balancing a slice of cheese pizza skillfully on his head our Nonna has shown that God is not only resourceful in the face of adversity, but also compassionate as he looks for survivors to share his snack with. We are saddened at the thought of the disappearance of what was rumored to be her greatest work - a still life painting of a bowl of her homemade linguini covered with a melting of Cheez Whiz… luscious, greasy and dripping with old world goodness.

K.L.

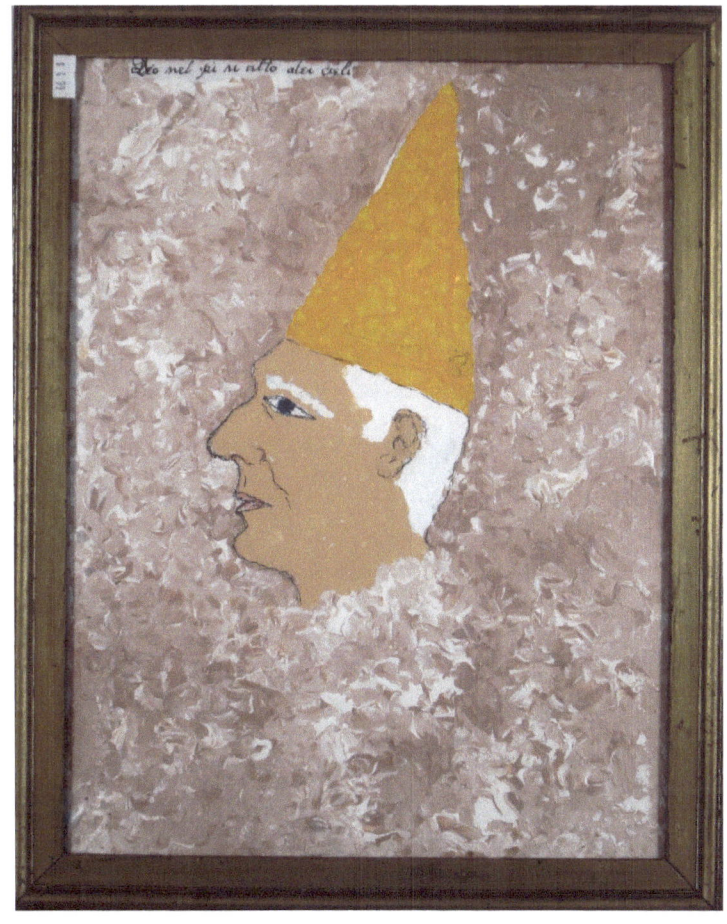

"Fatberg Floater"
Sir Hugh Manatee, 2013
Plumbago # 2 on yellowed carbonate gangue

The artist, Sir Hugh Manatee, is the United Kingdom's preeminent artist/environmentalist and here we see one of his latest contributions to the ongoing battle of England's sewer repair workers against fatbergs. This 15 tonne, 80 meter long, massive mountain of congealed fat and wet wipes had clogged a sewer pipe in south-west London. In a delicate pencil rendering of an indelicate subject matter, Sir Manatee was the first to artistically document the societal results of England's love affair with bacon fat and clean bottoms. This is a call to all members of the wet wipe community (one in five loo goers) to cease and desist their mindless habits of obsessive edulcorating so that these "nasty solid messes" will in time, find an infamous niche in urban mythology alongside the woman who dried her toy poodle in a microwave oven.

K.L. and D.S.

"Route 66 Beans and Beef"
Buck Merritt, 1955
Mierda de vaca and salsa on stretched bull scrotums

This is an original work by part-time truck driver, bull castrator, and truck stop menu designer, Buck Merritt. We are drawn to this downsized landscape because of Merritt's practical use of found materials to create his menu cover illustrations. The artist has faithfully portrayed the yearly migration of well behaved New Mexican ash trees as they arrange themselves in orderly lines and march quietly over the hill - We are also impressed by the numerological use of 3 mesas, 5 rocks, 10 trees, 13 chilies, and 200 white dots… what that all means, we have absolutely no idea.

K.L.

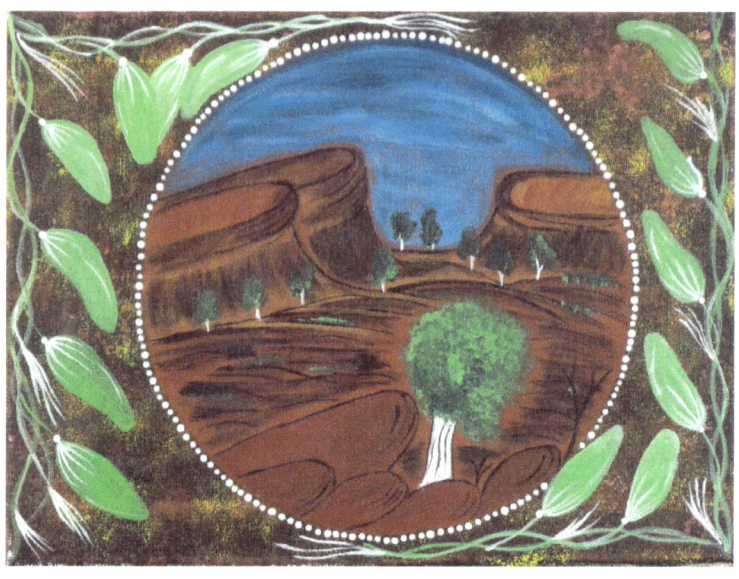

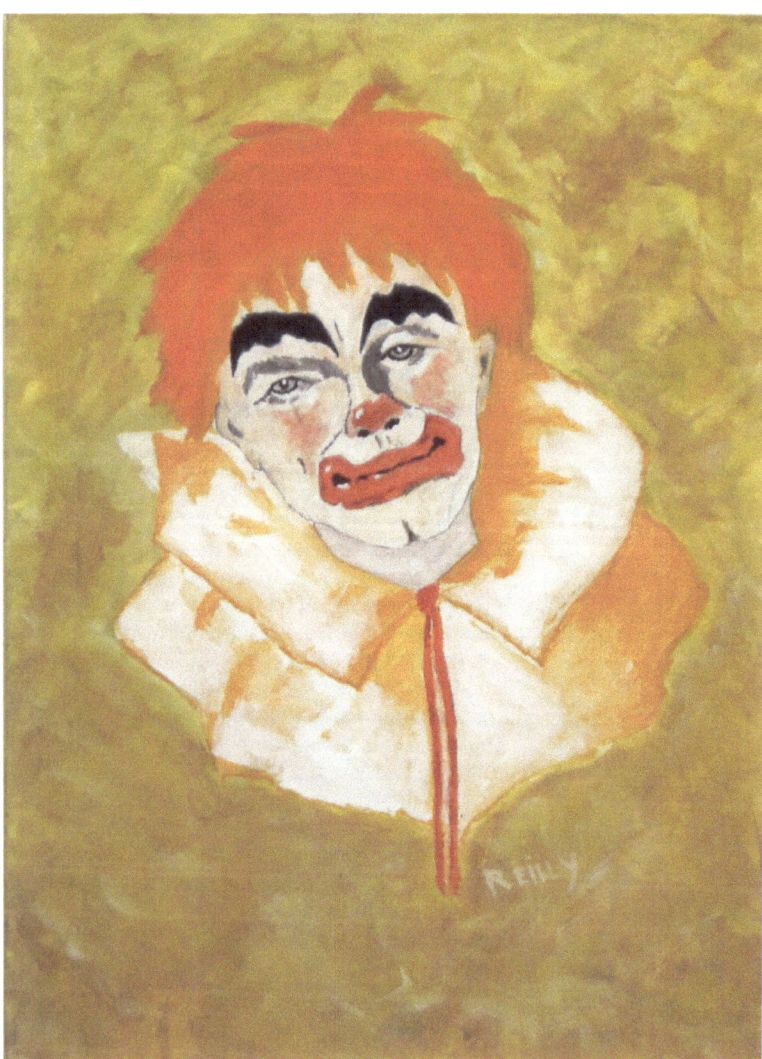

"Every child is an artist. The problem is how to remain an artist once we grow up."
- Pablo Picasso

"Po-Po Hits the Wall"
Nixie Reilly, 2001
An infusion of mashed carrot tea on Brawny Paper Towels

The doctor had warned Po-Po against a strict, carrots-only diet, but being a clown, he just laughed it off.

K.L.

12

"Empyrean Surf Queen"
Columbina Amidine aka Lebism, 1998
Acrylic on canvas

Here we see a cosmic surfing goddess serenely hanging 10 on the majestic purple waves of an everlasting curl. They surge and roll beneath her feet as the earth peeps like a voyeur from an infinite sea of atmospheric churning. Proudly wearing her flamboyant feather boa like a Las Vegas showgirl, she holds a shark zapper stick thingy and displays a glass-fronted washing machine in her abdomen. It seems that the waters of this artistic vision are very deep indeed.

K.L.

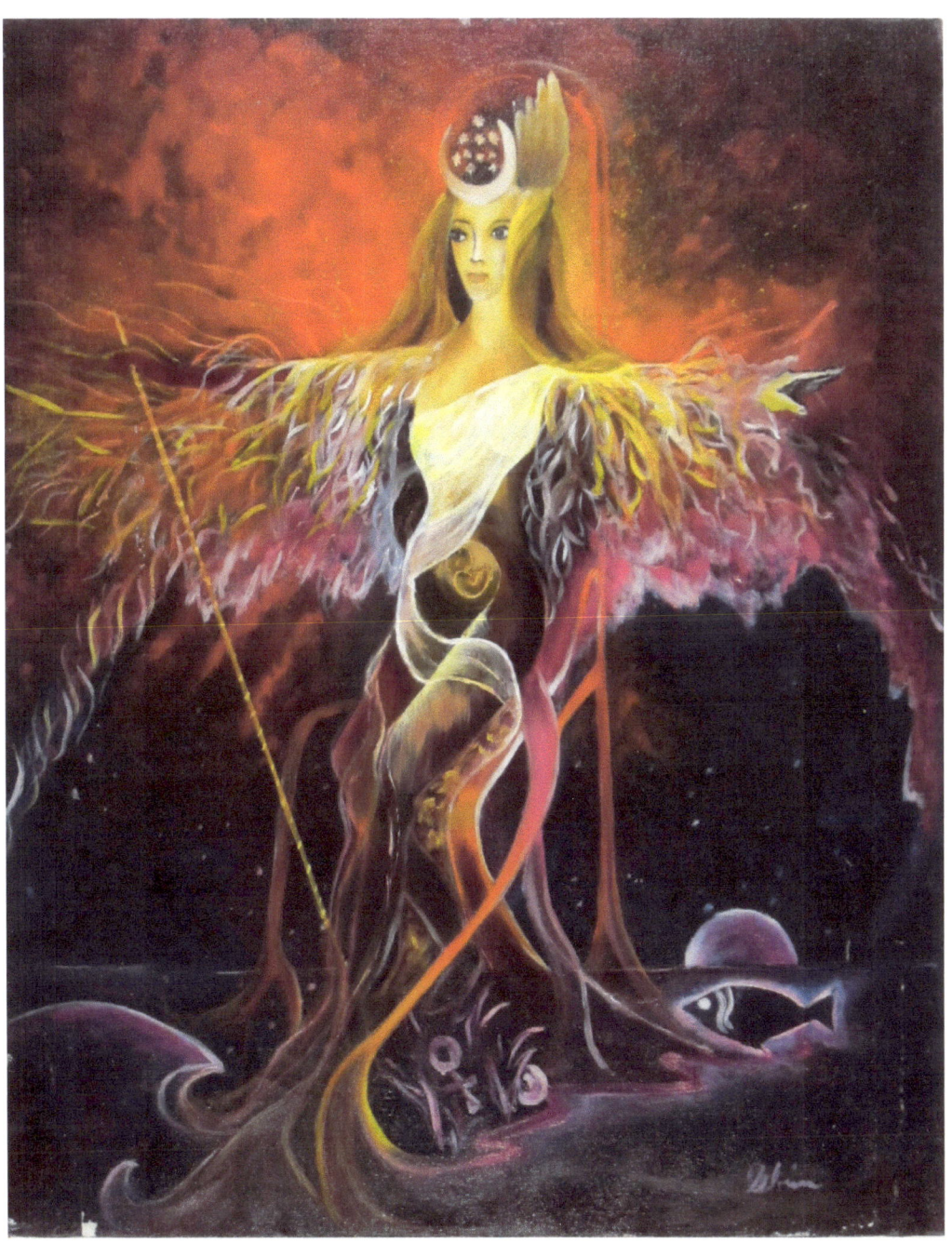

"Art is the daughter of freedom."   - Friedrich Schiller

13

"Until the End of the World"
Eric Oneiric, 2007
*Acrylic paint applied with a great moaning and
gnashing of teeth, kidney sourced egesta, bitter
tears from a holy wellspring*

This intriguing and architecturally robust piece was
created following the artist's near death
experience from a head injury on an amusement
park ride. When asked to explain this work, he
said that these were recently passed souls who
had marched from the shores of Tripoli and were
headed to the halls of Montezuma. He had used a
lot of yellow to represent their need to pee but
they couldn't because they were in Purgatory for
the expiation of their earthly sins. They'd never
reach the bathrooms and they couldn't pee behind
the pillars because St. Peter was keeping an eye
on them and would cast them into hell if he caught
them. Above them on the arching structures is
where the pure souls went on a fast track to
heaven, which was in the tall towers in the
background.

K.L.

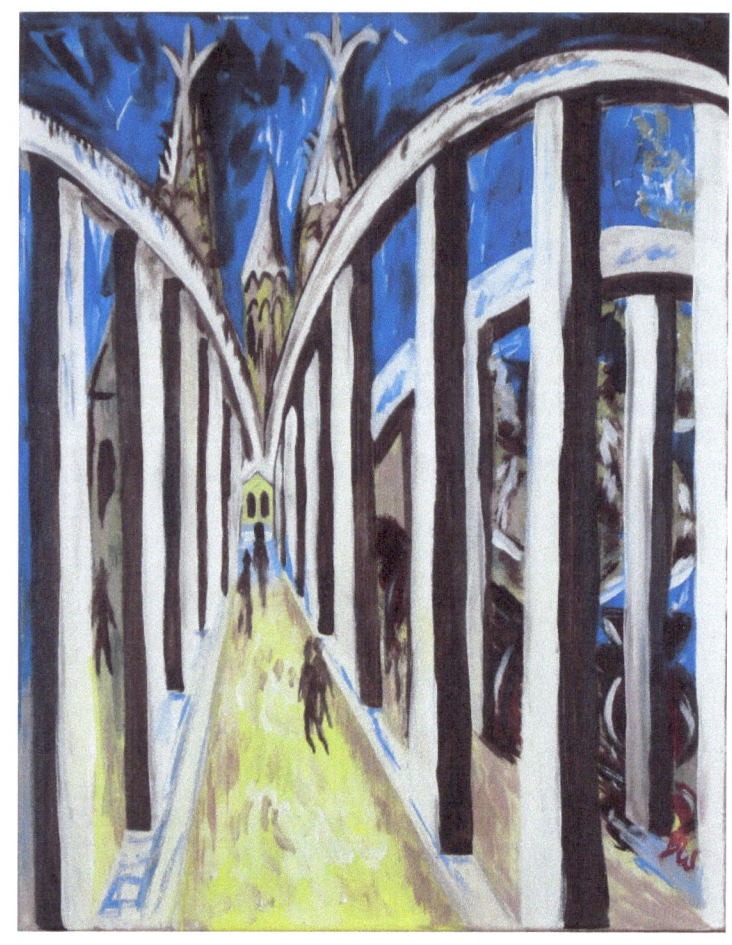

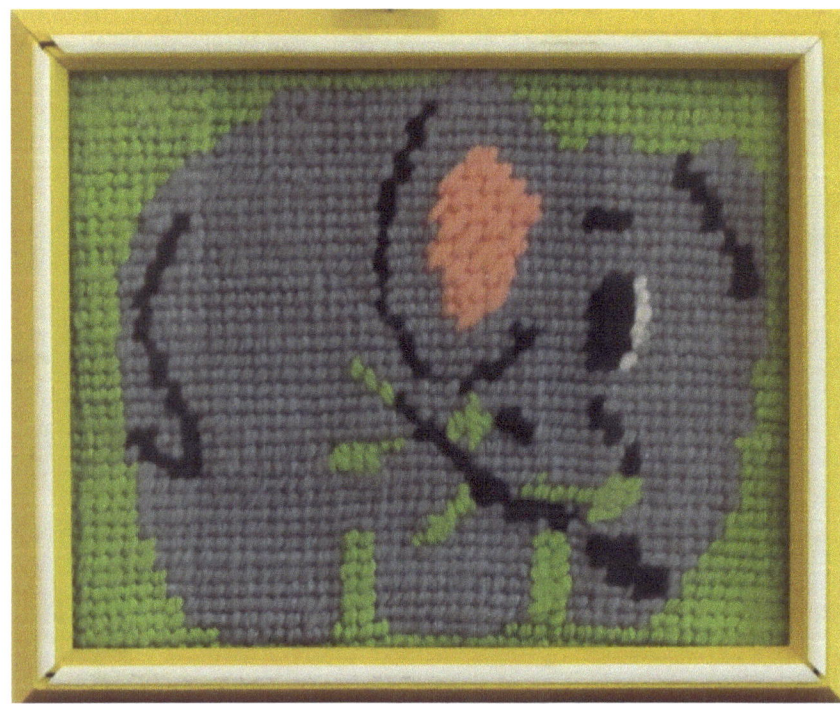

"Adorable Dumbo"
Jane Justice Smith, 1990
Polyester yarn on canvas

We applaud this charming little piece
woven so meticulously and snugly tucked
into its festive yellow frame! It faithfully
carries on the time-honored tradition we
humans uphold of turning wild animals
into loveable, cuddly creatures. This
miniature pachyderm joins its brothers,
the grizzly cubs, baby pandas, koala
bears, sea otters, lion and tiger cubs as
well as ducklings and wolf pups in a long
line of animals we just love to love. We
give it a "10" on the luvbug meter and
bonus points for the sturdy polyester yarn
used in its creation - a yarn that will last
long past the time when the only
elephants alive will be those in zoos. How
fortunate we are to have these adorable
images to remember them by!

K.L.

14

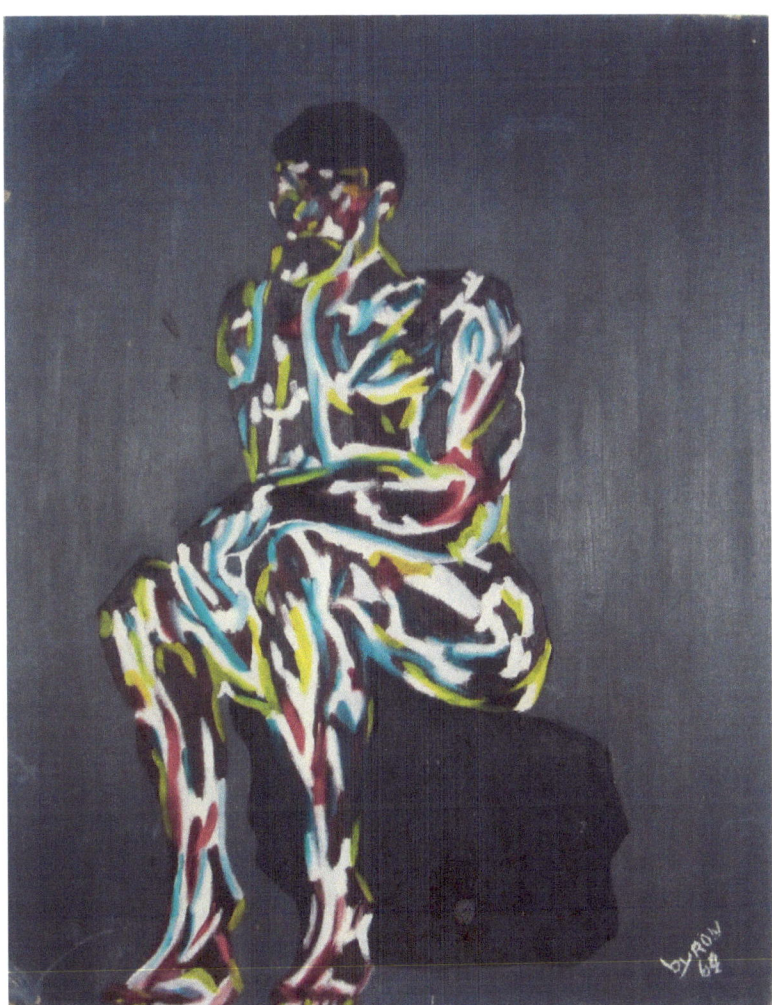

"Pondering a Movement"
Ron, 1964
Acrylic on board

Let's face it. Being human means occasionally having your intestines freeze up. You try drinking lots of water and maybe a bunch of prunes and finally you get desperate and take a little pill to get it all moving again. And while you wait for the pill to take effect you decide to get naked and do a little introspection. And wouldn't you know it, once you start your soul-searching, all your subtle energetic anatomy fields get activated, start to zap and glow all over your body and of course this attracts attention especially when you do it on a rock, at night, in your front yard. A passerby snaps a picture before he calls the police, but we're glad he did because now we have indisputable proof that subtle energetic anatomy fields actually exist and a lovely painting to illustrate them. We're guessing the laxative went to work around the time our obstructed sophist was being booked at the police station.

K.L.

"Hunting in Botswana"
Epsilon Chi Nu, 2000
Acrylic on board

We are so excited to have our first pointillist piece for our collection! Not since George Seurat and Paul Signac have we seen such masterly application of paint, which invites the viewer's eye and mind to blend the color spots into a fuller range of tones. On this small, but powerful canvas the conscious juxtaposing of red and yellow dots skillfully captures the life and death struggle between a 750lb wildebeest and a ferocious African lion. The herd escapes in the distance as more lions close in to make the kill. When not being viewed by throngs of Impressionist revivalists, the painting does double duty as a festive cheese grater for pasta nights or 20 grit sand paper, good for removing stubborn heel calluses.

K.L.

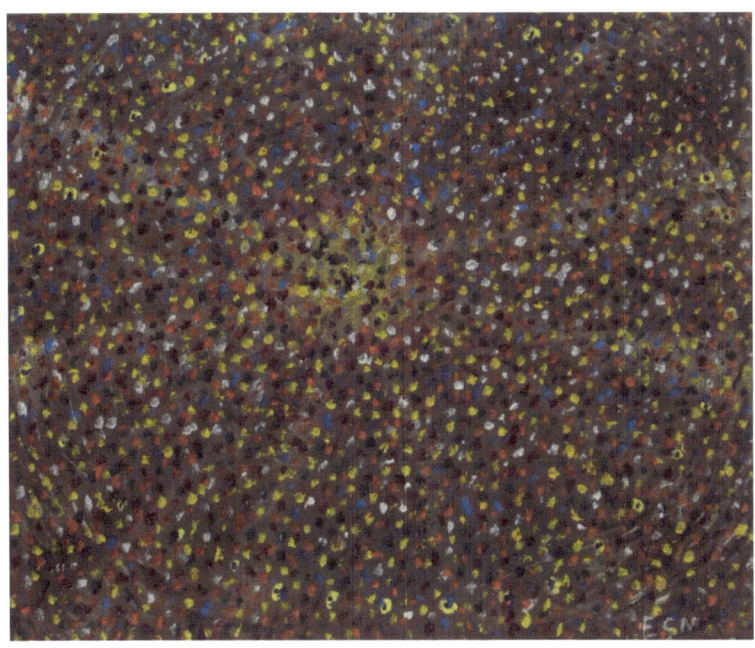

"Muppets On Meth"
Zizi Buzzinsky, 2013
Acrylic on dirty bed sheet

K.L.

"Art is born of humiliation."
- W. H. Auden

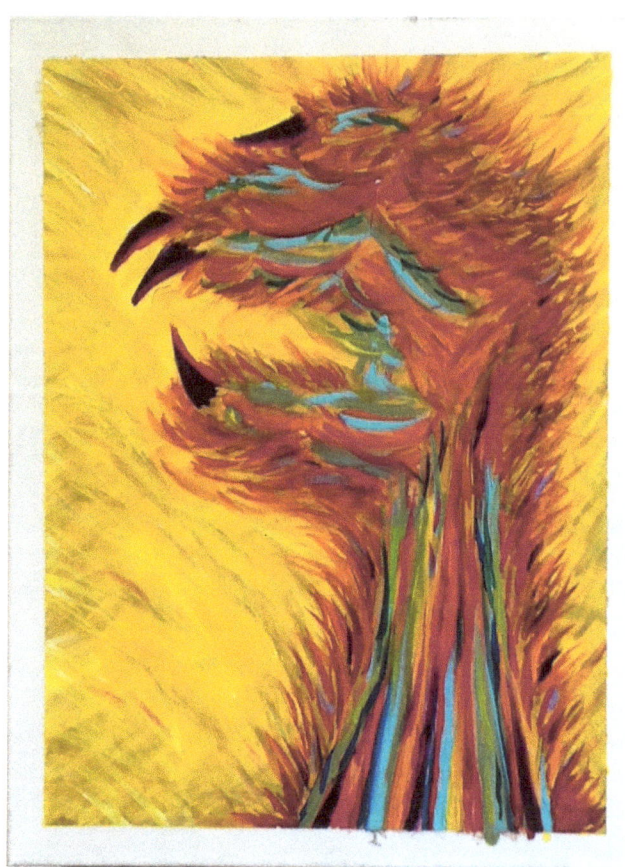

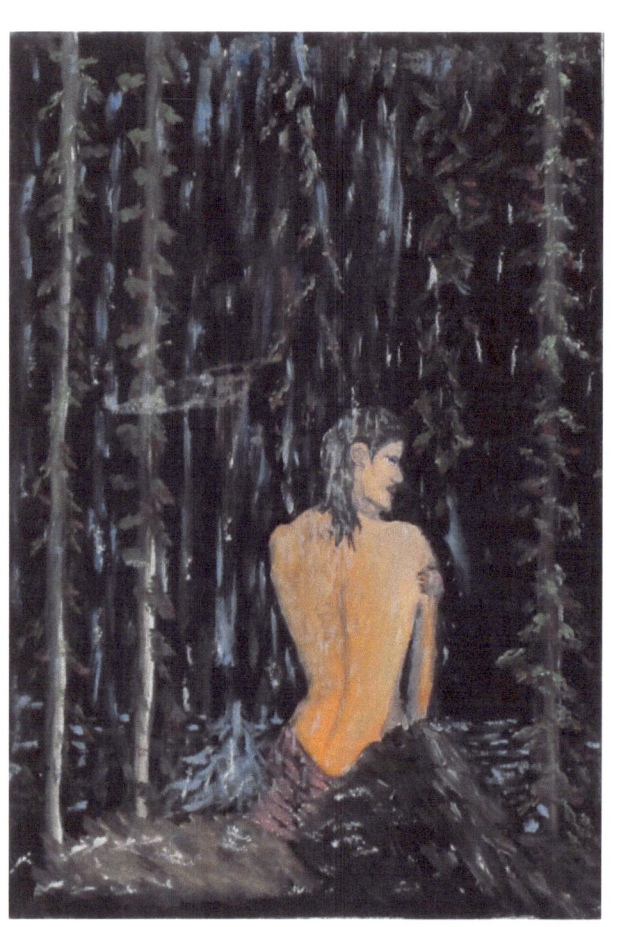

"Maiden In the Waterfall"
Amorexia Lovelorn, 2002
Acrylic on canvas

In this homage to the great William-Adolphe Bouguereau, the artist Lovelorn has recreated a timeless mood of sylvan seclusion as the wide shouldered nymph waits expectantly for her wild satyr to arrive. Fresh from the salon her graceful hand glistens with crimson tips. Tonight the forest will echo with the cries of sensuality and forbidden love.

K.L.

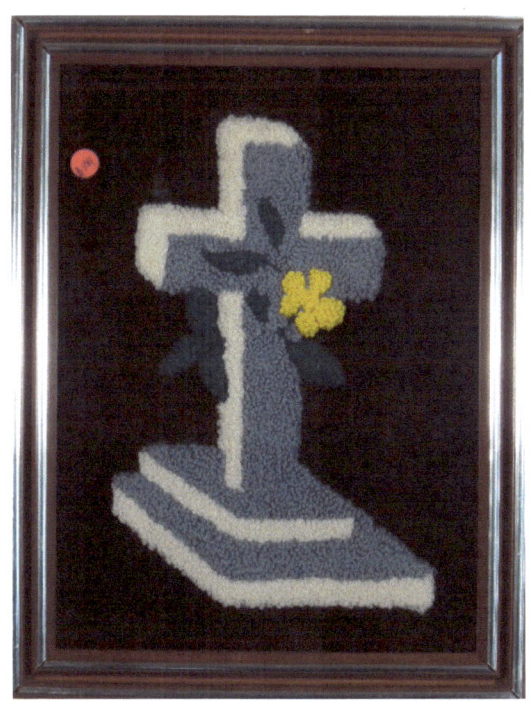

"God Bless Poppy"
Gwelda Huckabee and Friends, 1960
Black Velvet, Poodle fur

Gwelda Huckabee's happy hookers coffee klatch created this handcrafted treasure as an outpouring of their grief at the loss of Gwelda's bag-o-bones poodle Poppy. With expert attention given to detail, perspective and botanical accuracy, a more talented gathering of Iowan farm ladies could not be found. Hanging on little Poppy's grave in the pet cemetery for decades it was barely rescued from the destructive scoop of an earth grader preparing the land for a strip mall. Rumored that the grey yarn used in the piece was spun from Poppy's fur, on days when humidity is high the faint odor of doggie breath emanates from this touching farm town eulogy.

K.L.

"The Dewlips Method"
Freeman Dewlips, 2012
Acrylic on canvas

Having denied himself sleep for 9 days and existing on nothing but high colonic enemas of espresso and Tropical Punch Gatorade, our artist has created this unique work of unparalleled vision. Dewlips used a double fisted approach to his work, thereby doubling his output and perhaps pioneering a new technique in contemporary painting. The resulting piece emanated from a netherworld demesne where complete physical breakdown and creative output had merged. When asked how he accomplished such a beautiful landscape he said, "I did it just to find out what kind of crazy shit I would see. It was like earth sounds that came out of my pelvic chakra– all jacked up and glowing like wild terra vibes coming right at me, man. And it told me man, that it's going on all the time and we just don't know it. This shit is real man! And I have this painting to prove it. Even the little trees know it, cause they are tuned into the vibes too. They're all going like, 'Whoa! What's happening here? Our photosynthesis is peakin' man!' Sometimes it felt like I was channeling for van Gogh - you know, man, all his colors and little houses and farms and shit."

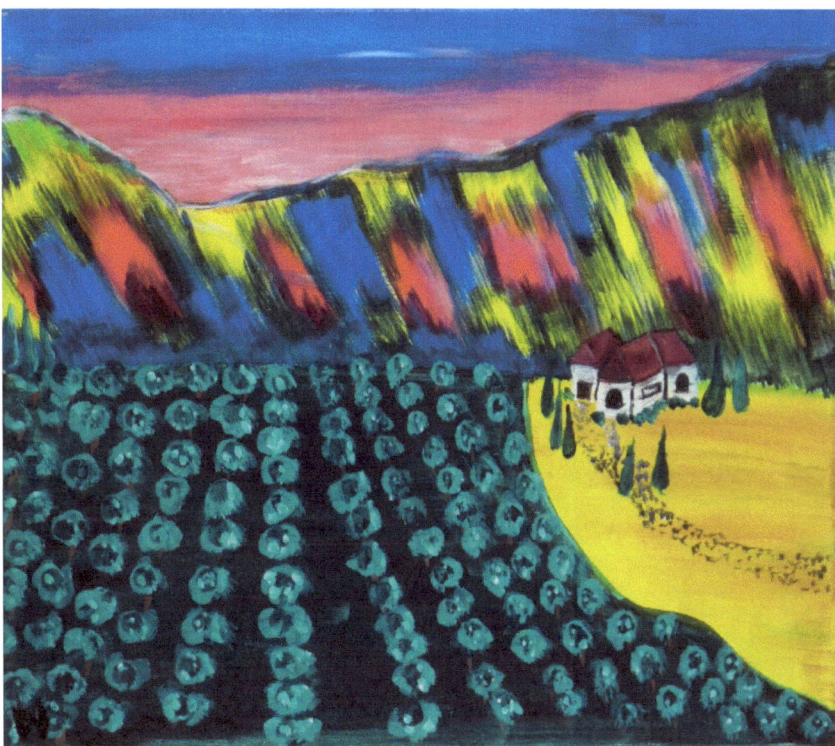

K.L.

"Breastfeeding Grandpa"
Camaro Blue, 1975
Oil on Masonite

Initially we are drawn into the dark, mysterious depths of this piece because like most viewers we are fascinated by babies and boobies, especially when the infant looks like the mom's leering grandfather. Lacking the courage to look directly at the aberration in her arms, the mother lowers her eyes. Is she considering shoving him back onto the fiery tube from whence he came? Perhaps Blue fears his own mother felt this way or maybe he wishes he had breasts to feed himself. Some say the artist is exploring issues of gender identity and nurturing while examining his helpless old man dwarf side.

K.L.

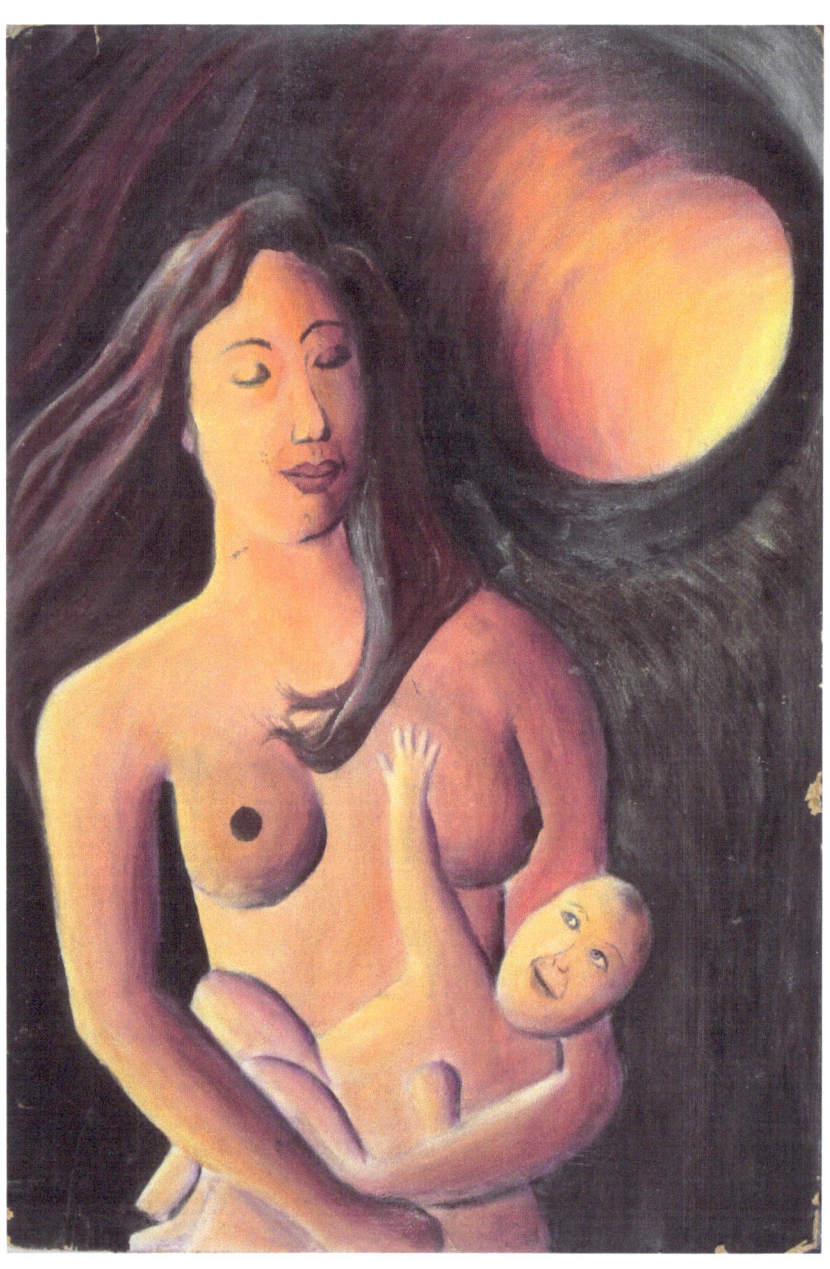

"If you hear a voice within you say 'you cannot paint,' then by all means paint, and that voice will be silenced." - Vincent Van Gogh

"The Uptown Train"
Bikyerd Smith, 2013
Pneumo toxic pastel on paper

The subway train is late again. Commuters are in various stages of anxiety and frustration. Five have disintegrated into dusty little poofs of color. The air conditioning is broken so everyone has understandably taken off their clothes. The train is nowhere in sight and the tracks have vanished. The artist paints himself as a helpless torso in agonized supplication, beseeching the subway authorities to send a train soon -- or at least a big earthworm for them to ride to their next exit. But, in the distance blind and squeaking, a giant Sub-Saharan Mole Rat moves toward them. The situation looks bleak.

K.L.

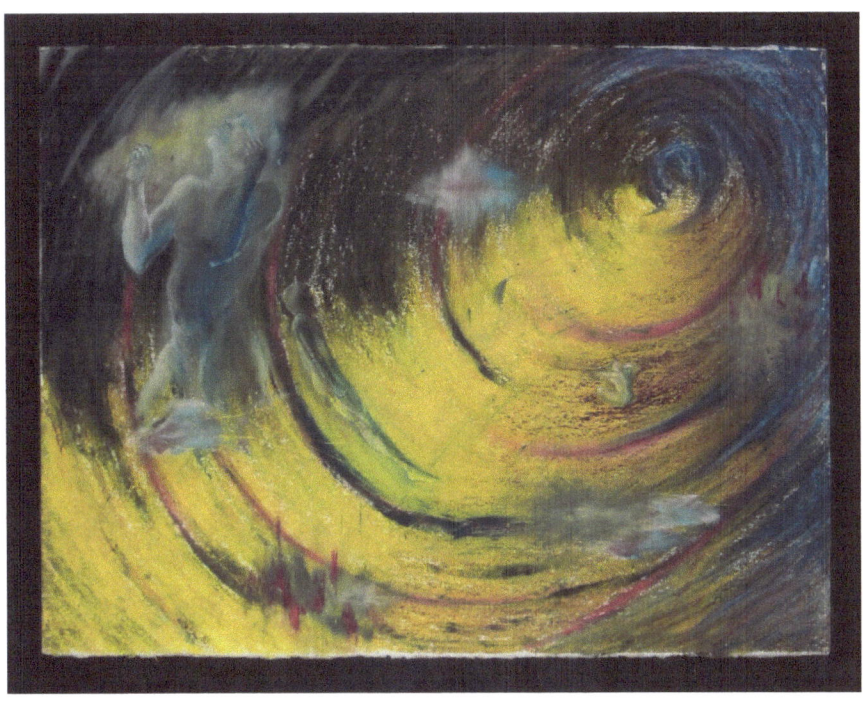

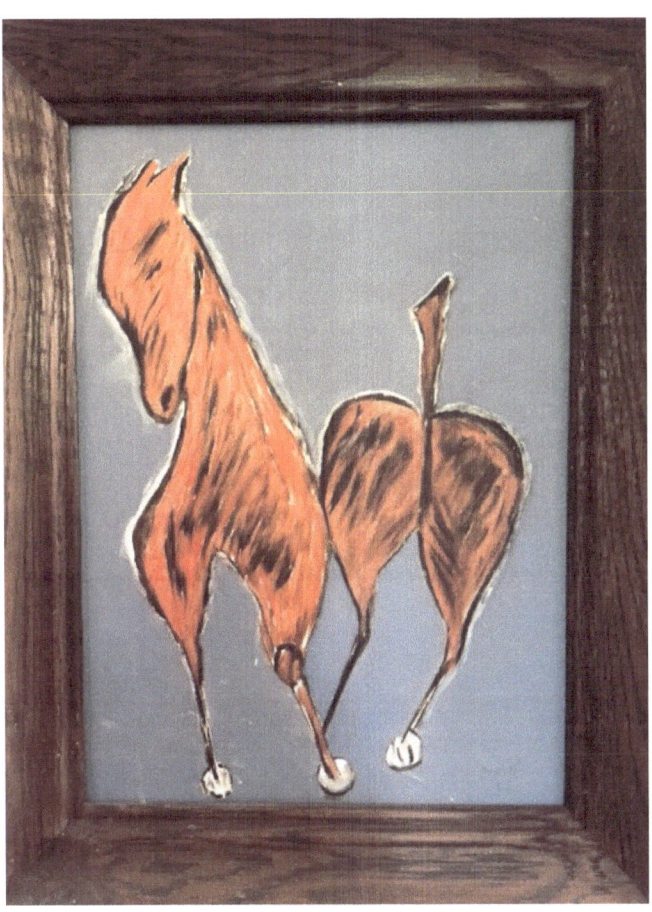

"Farewell to Kaseem"
Windham Thomas Wyndham - Quinn, the 4th Earl of Dunraven, 1898
Orange grease pencil and charcoal on Irish slated limestone with hand rubbed black walnut frame

We treasure this fine piece characterized by its strong neotenous quality. Created by the 4th Earl of Dunraven when he was just 18 years old, it depicts his beloved recently deceased Arabian stallion, Kaseem, after a botched taxidermy job. Sadly, this painting is the only record that remains of the great stud after the stuffed specimen was attacked and devoured by a plague of dermestid beetles in London's Museum of Natural History. You may ask how we came to possess this Victorian jewel, but we must occasionally protect our sources.

K.L.

"Lake Merced Reflections"
Trey Just Trey aka Trey Trey, 2012
Oil on canvas board

When he's not jerking $7 coffees for "some rich techie asshole" in SOMA, hipster icon, Trey Trey, depicts an introspective moment in his ironically lived life. Having let his man bun down he perfects his hipster hunch and contemplates his fashion future. Is he considering ditching his tight, effortlessly cool corduroy pants, button up shirt and bowtie for the bare foot Iron Age retro toga look? We love Trey Trey's rebelliously wielded 1950s pastel paint by number style and lush use of patterns and textures that flirt with the style of the great Fauvist landscape painters of the past. Do we dare call his work the dernier cri of this genre?

K.L.

"Art stirs the soul and fills the spaces where words cannot go."
- Alexander Mayhew Olson

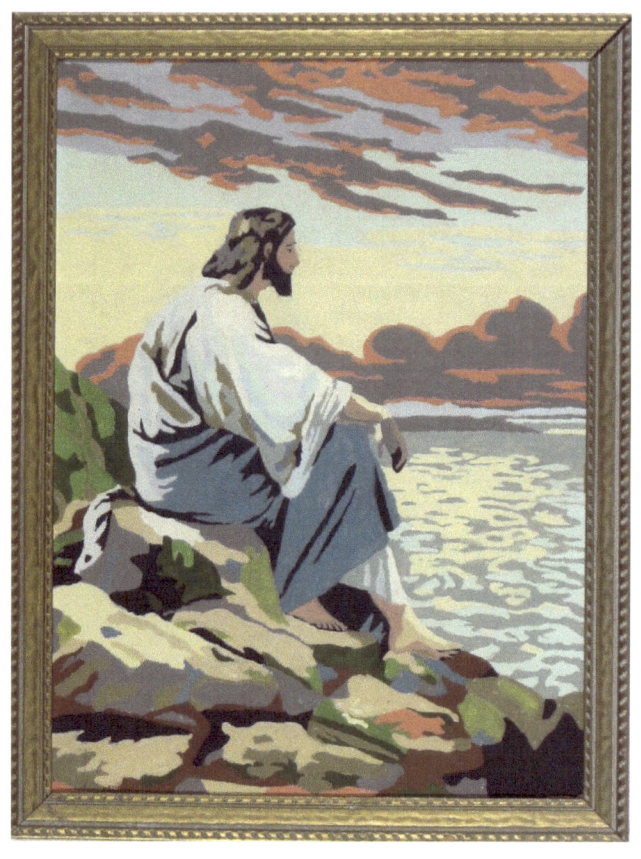

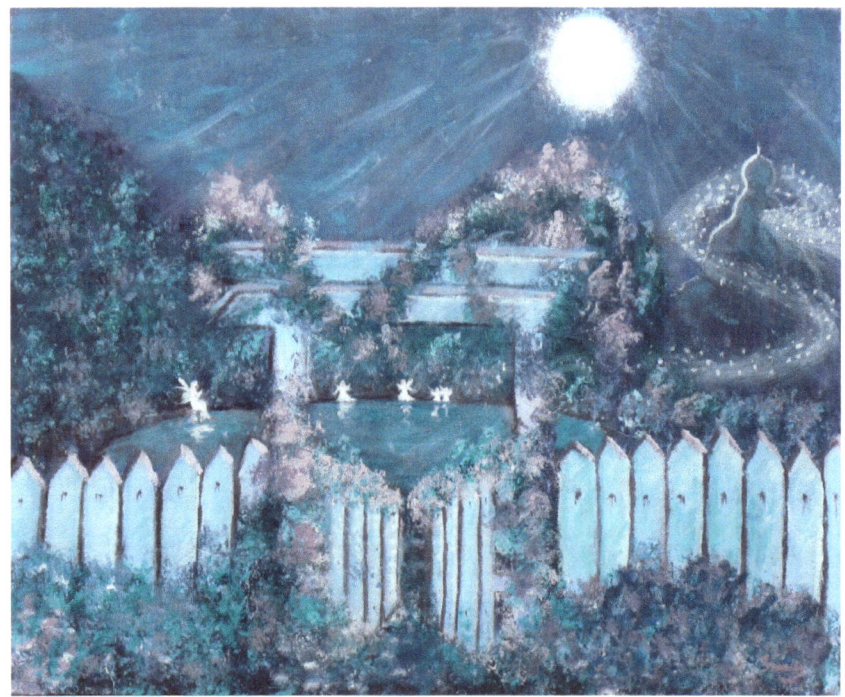

"Moon Palace Massacre"
Sanndy, 1999
Acrylic on canvas panel

In a violet-soft world of enchanting moonlight, thousands of fluttering fairies are entranced by flute music as they swarm on a silvery path to their own death and destruction. At the Moon Palace Fairy Cakes Factory they are stunned in bug zappers, freeze-dried and compressed into savory little crackers. The target market for this sinister new product is San Francisco's trendy Mission district wine bars and restaurants where they are spread with olive tapenade and paired with the finest of charcuteries and delicious Loire Valley wines. In this, her clarion call to action, the artist implores us to look at our shameful lifestyle luxuries and amend our appetites accordingly... "The horror! The horror!" Sanndy exclaims. "Save the fairies!"

K.L.

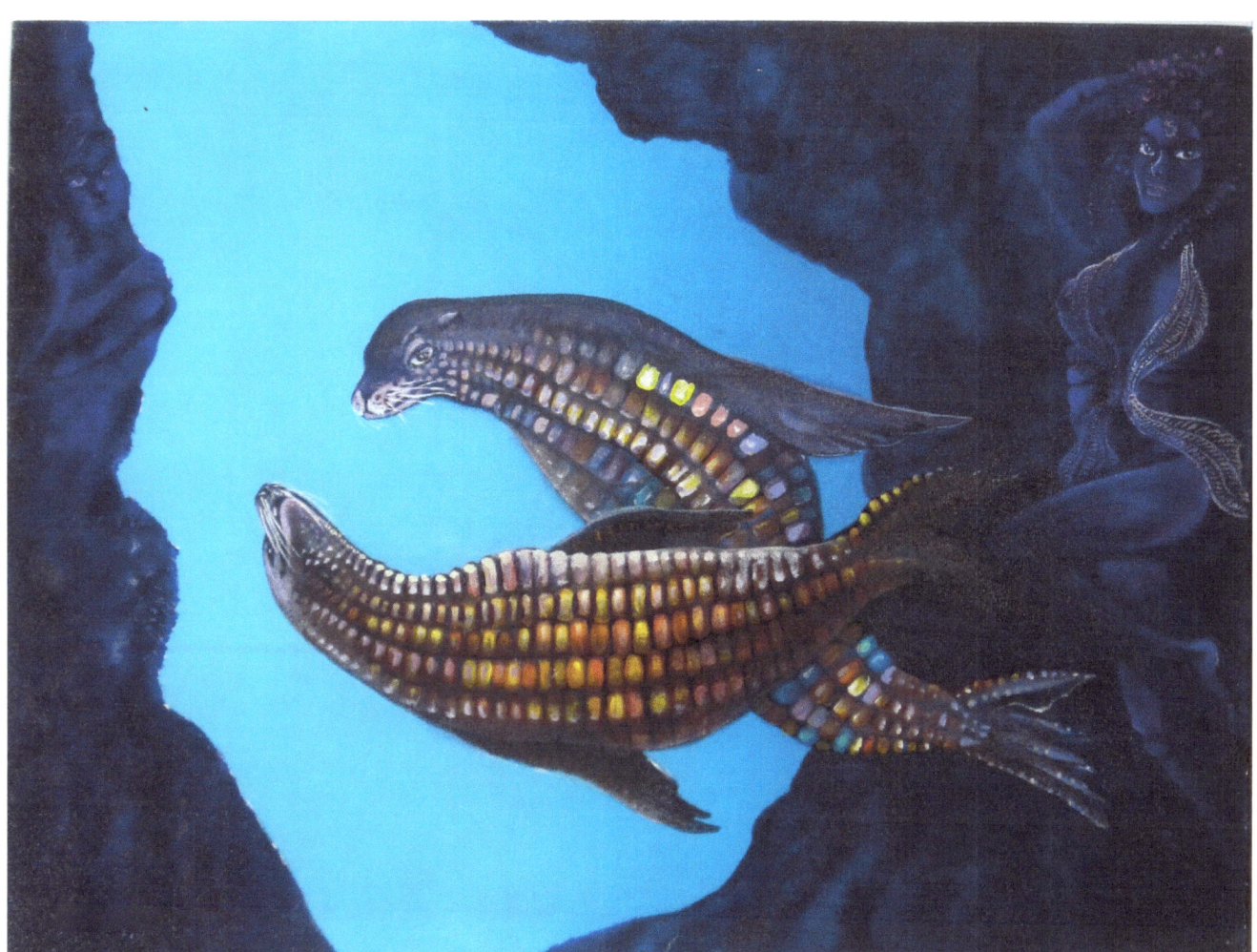

"Voodoo Realism"
Artist Unknown, 2007
Acrylic on canvas

Don't worry dear viewer if this unsettling piece, like fingernails on a blackboard, sets your teeth on edge and your mind spinning in confusion. Our unknown artist, with undeniably advanced skill, having been on a trash pickup on the roadside of his mind, has thrown together the ideas he found there and unleashed them on an unsuspecting public. One unfortunate creature looks out at us with disgusted boredom as if to say, " Can you believe what this guy has done to us? We look like escapees from a gmo lab experiment gone badly awry!" We can't tell if they are fun loving sea lions frolicking in the tropical water or ears of corn ready to be roasted, smeared with butter, and sprinkled with salt, pepper and a squeeze of limejuice. And of course when an artist loses his way in the storey telling, it's always good to goose the viewer with a few time honored gratuitous sex symbols lurking like purple submarine pole dancers. This painting recalls an old art instructor's words of advice: "creating art and recreational drugs should not be mixed…ever."

K.L.

"Of course you will say that I ought to be practical and ought to try and paint the way they want me to paint. Well, I will tell you a secret. I have tried and I have tried very hard, but I can't do it. I just can't do it! And that is why I am just a little crazy."
                                        - Rembrandt

"Gnome Baby Poser"
Dottie Dhurna, 1910
Elastomeric Stucco on canvas

This one of a kind historic piece was fortuitously rescued from the trash dumpster of a lawn gnome retirement community on the outskirts of Columbus, Ohio. It is believed to be a childhood portrait of the famous garden dwarf revolutionary leader, Duci Dhurna, who was known for his command of their nationwide militant strike in the mid to late 1930's. Protesting against the cruel harassment and outright disdain directed at them, their issues included, but were not limited to: dogs urinating on them, being left outside during inclement weather, forced to wear peeling coats of paint, dressed up as racial stereotypes and tp'd by drunken teenagers. This demeaning portrait of baby Duci shows him clothed in work boots, white tights and clown hat as he wistfully dreams of better times when all gnomes will unite to throw off the chains of lawn kitsch servitude and proudly join the works of the great sculptors such as Rodin, Michelangelo and X Martin Schambley III.

K.L.

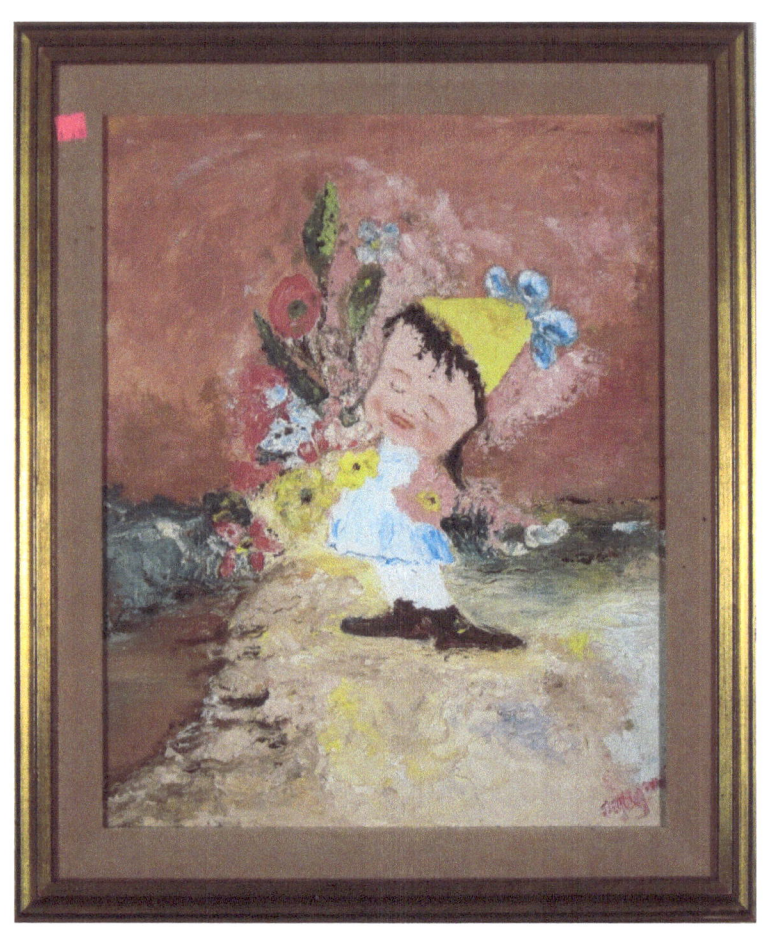

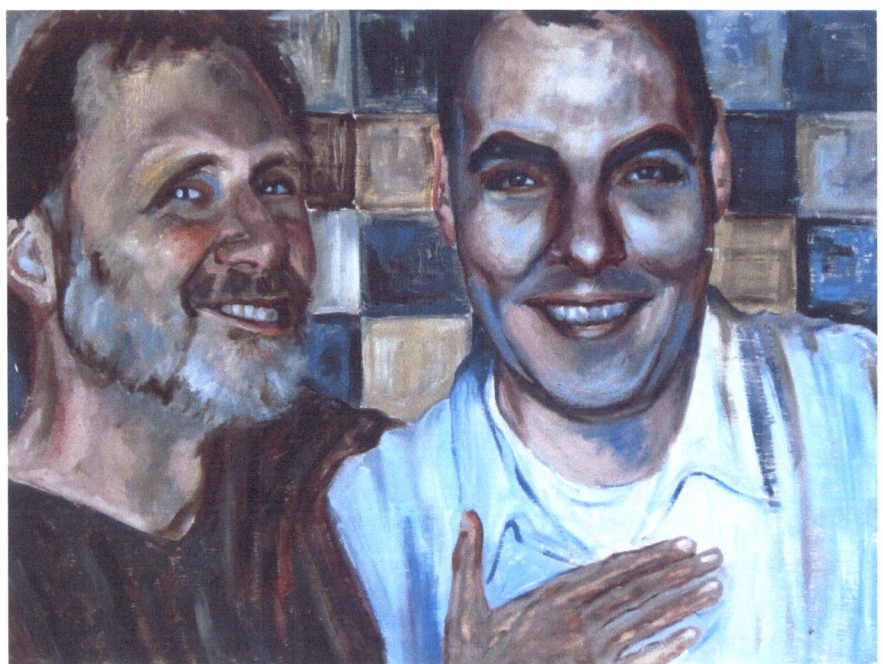

"I Want to Pet the Rabbit, George"
John Bickford Safety, 2004
Oil on board

Renowned self taught painter, Bickford Safety's, modern reimagining of the Steinbeck novel "Of Mice and Men" bleeds emotion and captures the striking smile of the devilishly handsome stranger in blue (George) and his slow witted bearded companion (Lenny). The artist has captured the carefree innocence of idiocy in the slack jaw and prominent forehead, while his dashing handler on the right exudes a dark mystery from eyes that seem to follow the viewer across the room. One can almost imagine the graying halfwit mouthing the words " Do I get to pet the rabbits now, George?"

Kevin Jones

"Portrait of the Artist's Nonna"
Bruno Monzano, 1956
Pratley's putty – colored globulitic type shot from a can

Neither impasto nor pointillist, this piece was executed with a brand new technique created by Manzano in honor of his beloved Nonna. Using a giant Cool Whip can the artist shot globulitic Pratley's Putty from 10 feet away, carefully building up layer upon layer of hard bumpy lumps. As Queen of the waste management business after her husband was whacked, Nonna Manzano was known and respected by all in the days before RICO. The artist cherishes fond memories of his Nonna - the smell of baking biscotti and the sound of her basement sub machine gun practice.

K.L.

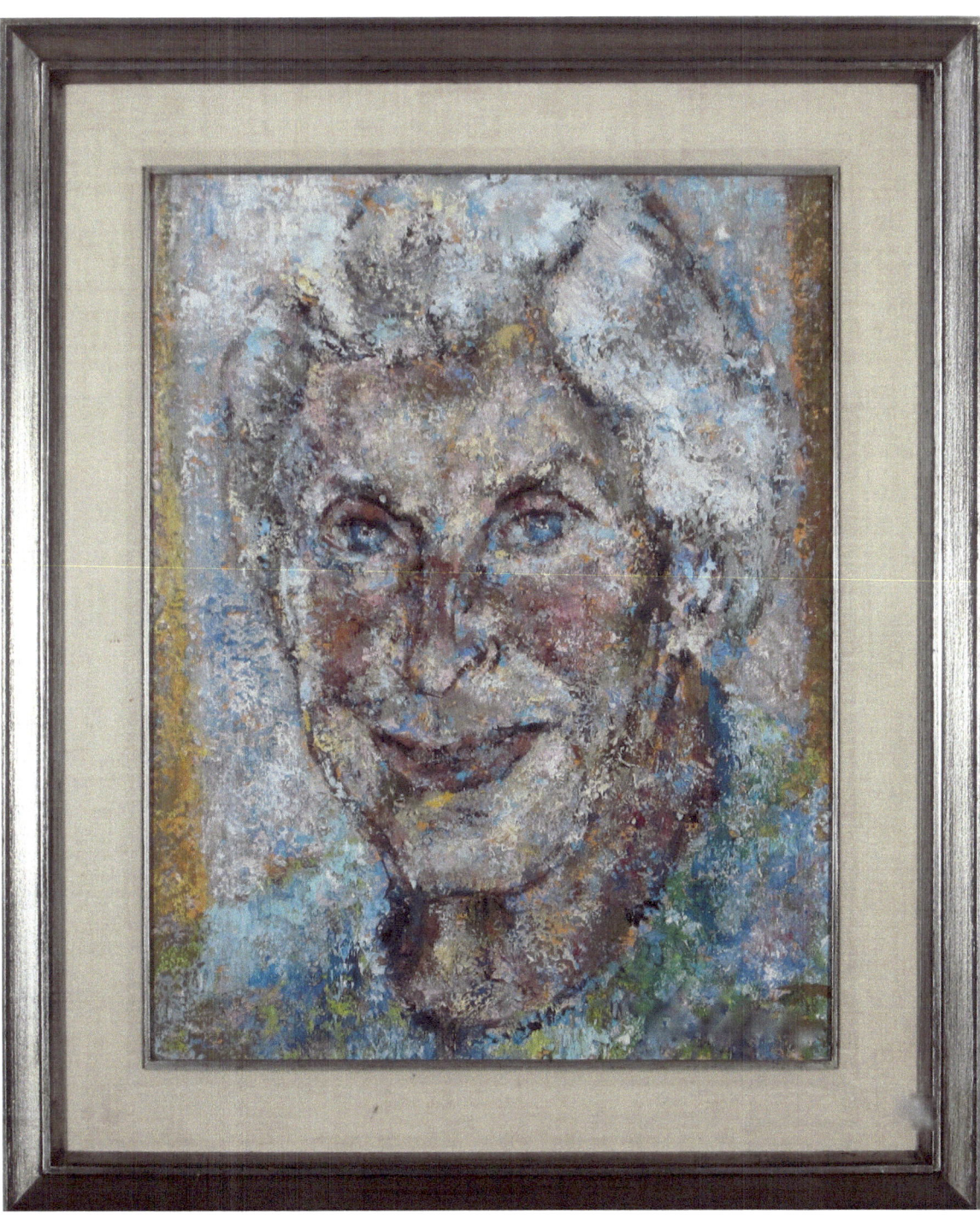

"Scallions in the Yoni Patch"
Ti. Fitzgerald, 2001
Acrylic on canvas

It is unclear whether these are arthritic green scallions or sexless Martian garden sprites that skip joylessly around the mint green diamond in Ti. Fitzgerald's feeble attempt at symbolism. The reoccurring diamond format seen in this painting recalls the artist's talentless career in major league baseball while the gaping blue center refers to the tremendous depression suffered, having never made it off the bench. This pathetic attempt at self-expression is hobbled by the basic blue green color theme on a bilaterally symmetrical canvas of simplistic boredom. It begs the question: Will he ever succeed at anything he does? Don't quit your day job, Ti. On Second thought, there may be a job for you writing shallow, meaningless Hallmark sympathy cards.

K.L.

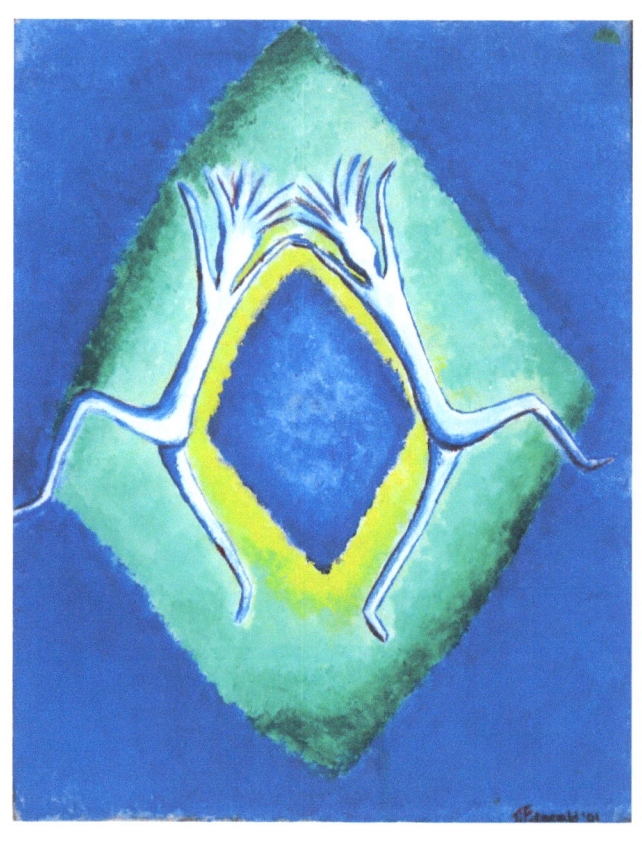

"The Agony of Brother Pippo / It Was His Bag Baby!"
Pippo Monolo, 1489
Organic pasta sauce and Hershey's chocolate syrup on calfskin

The eccentric, but gifted Italian Renaissance monk is famous for never having left his cozy, but highly flammable paper bag hut. On loan from the Vatican, we are privileged to have in our collection his final creation, produced while peering out at a fiery landscape and desperately chanting the Act of Contrition. This magnificent work born of such tragic circumstances survived the sweeping inferno in pristine condition. But alas! Br. Monolo's remains were anything but pristine. With blackened lips covered in chocolate syrup his charred corpse was found protectively clutching this testament to his chest. A marble shrine stands where his bag used to be; the magnificent old tree, long thought dead, is now crowned with leafy green and miraculously issues forth a bubbling spring from its base.

K.L.

24

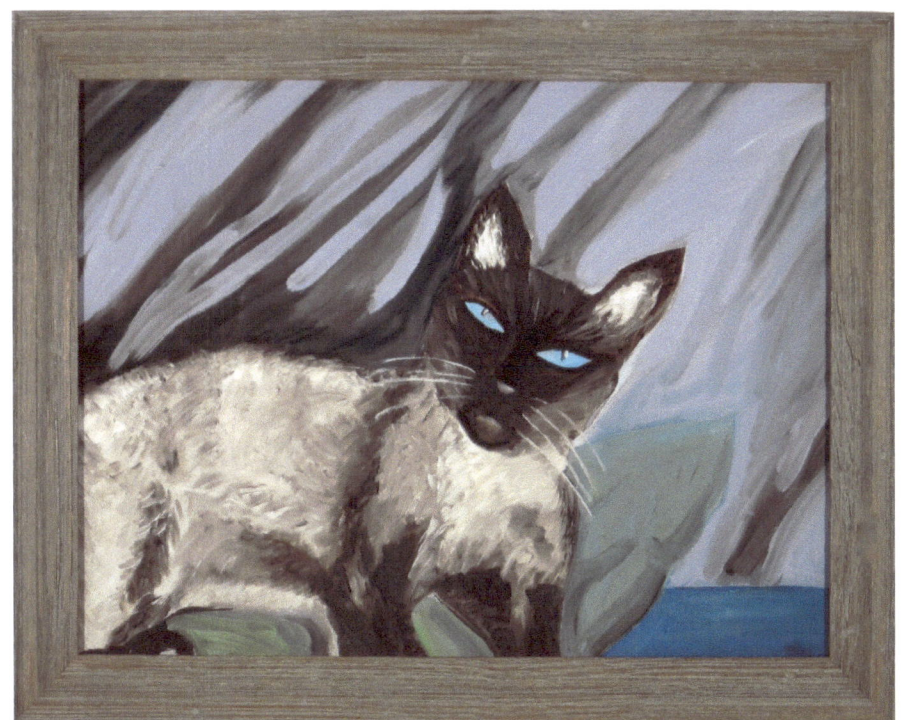

"The Exterminator"
Shinola Phelps, 1972
Acrylic on board

His fur looks soft, but his eyes are saying, "If you were just one tenth your size I would break your neck with a single bite and then just for fun toss your lifeless body into the air. Then I would eat your braincase or maybe just leave you for the blowflies. I've never loved you and I never will. That's right, I'm not your lickspittle doggie."

K.L.

"Painting is easy when you don't know how, but very difficult when you do."
-Edgar Degas

"Winkelpicker's Epiphany / Erections in the Sun"
Rutherford Winkelpicker, 2001
Acrylic on canvas board

In this deeply existential piece, the soon to be up and coming artist Rutherford Winkelpicker confronts the enormity of the realization that his existence means absolutely nothing to anyone, not even his mother or his dog. The resulting emotional tsunami threatens to sweep him from his little perch at the nude beach where he has gone, desperately searching for a quick hook-up. With expert brush strokes and masterly use of deep watery greens, luscious pinks and passionate purples Winkelpicker leaves the unsuspecting viewer speechless and gasping for the higher ground of emotional detachment… and worrying a bit too at the thought of his sunburned tender bits.

K.L.

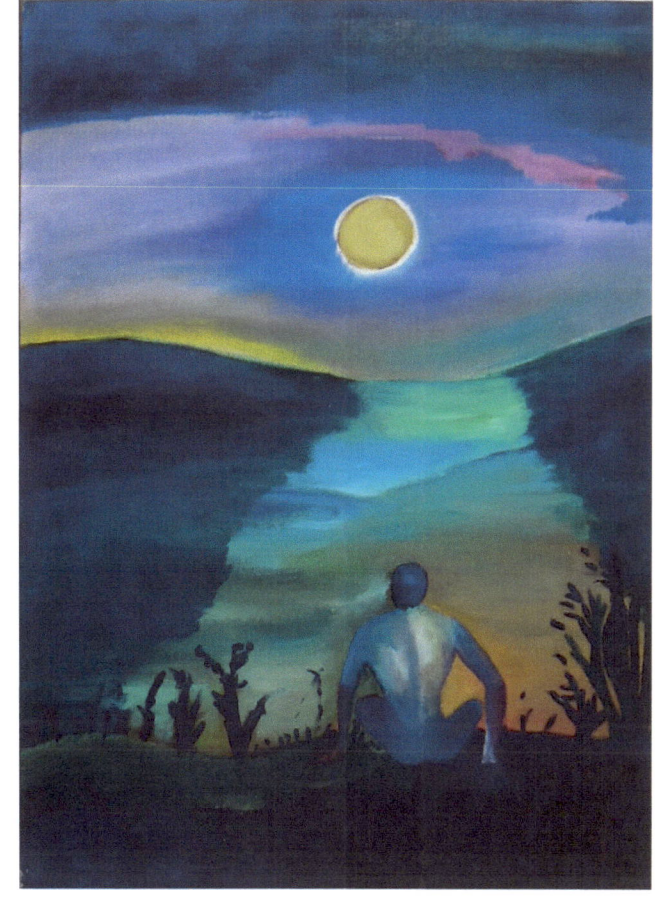

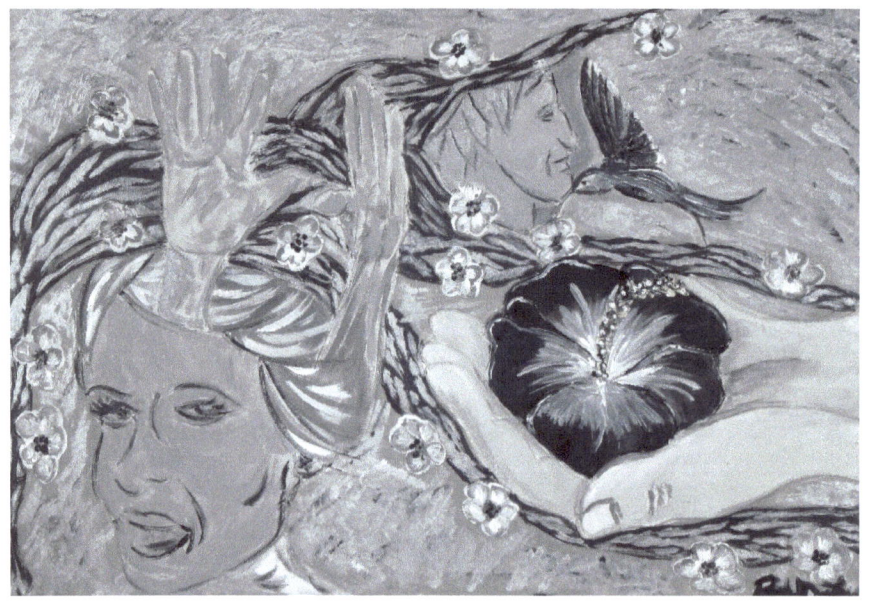

"Grey Has no Agenda"
Artist Unknown – well of course – who would admit to this?
Acrylic on canvas board

A disgusted Hibiscus queen is sick to death of supplicants bringing more flowers. Royal noggin hands held high, she gives the signal of all hibiscus queens to just basta! Please! A man in the background proudly displays his hummingbird chin ornament. Hope springs eternal as we look for meaning in this piece, but finally we are forced to admit that sometimes shit just happens.

K.L.

"The Pigeon Handler"
Jojo Cracko, 1998
Acrylic on canvas board

The legendary six-fingered fly by reach around (SFFBRA), depicted in this painting is the hottest topic at Millennial cocktail parties today. As a popular social commentator and spokesman for that generation, our artist Jojo Cracko wields his brush with a charm and devil may care know-how that immediately captivates and challenges even the indifferent art viewer. This particular type of SFFBRA sports two thumbs and gripping bird talons for any stabilization issues that may arise once the bucking starts. And for future research and study, Jojo has added a combined myopic eye/video camera nestled in the palm of the hand that can document a bird's eye view of the fleshy friction slip and slide. Ladies, be sure to keep a look out for this low flying bird that is ready to lend a neighborly helping hand to those in need.

K.L.

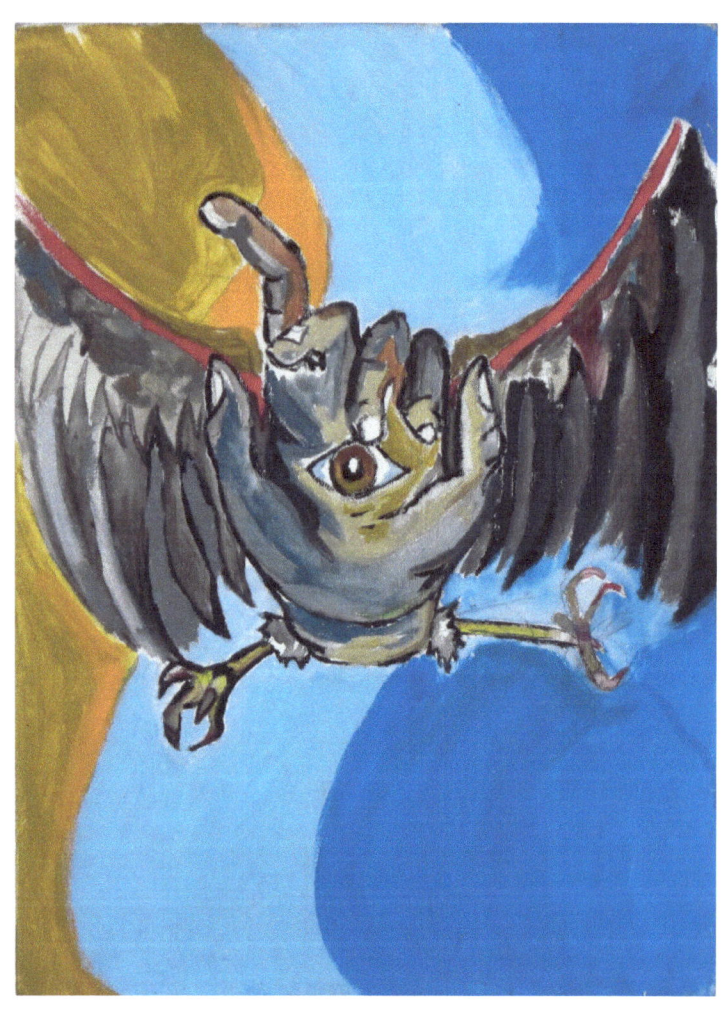

"A Core Memory For Crystal"
S. Morrow, 1978
Oil on canvas

A flock of small red flowers flutter protectively around this horribly sun burnt girl as blue delphiniums look on sympathetically. It seems that these are the only creatures that care two hoots about the worried little bench bound amputee. Where are her adults, why didn't they put some sunscreen on her and where is her wheel chair? She glances nervously to her right assessing her chances of a quick escape if a big hairy Sasquatch suddenly emerges from the forbidding woods behind her. Maybe he's the one who took her leg off. Maybe she's being used as bait so the adults can make a YouTube video of it. We see a psychiatrist couch in this child's future - if she makes it that far.

K.L.

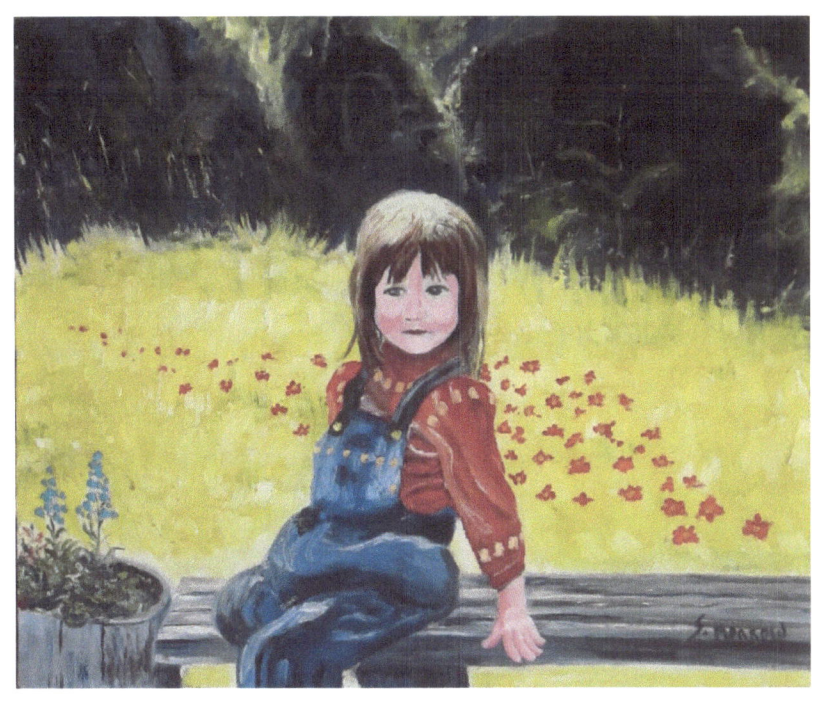

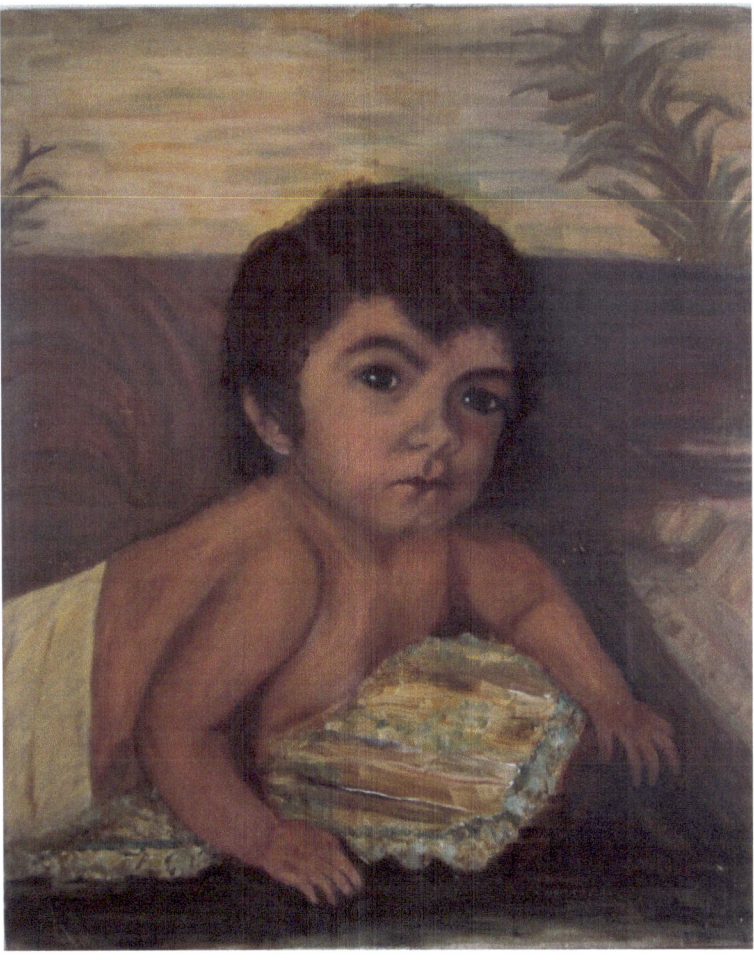

"Every artist was first an amateur."
- Ralph Waldo Emerson

"Baby Al"
Benedetto Di Parma, 1899
Oil on millboard

Julius Cesar, Hernan Cortes, and now Baby Al Capone -this child has definitely been around before. His manly face and commanding stare demand respect. The 19th century Brooklyn artist Di Parma, wielding a limited value range, demonstrates exquisite skill juxtaposing the murderous energy of a gangster larva reclining helplessly on a fluffy baby blanket. In a few years this infant would be declaring: "Now I know why tigers eat their young.

K.L.

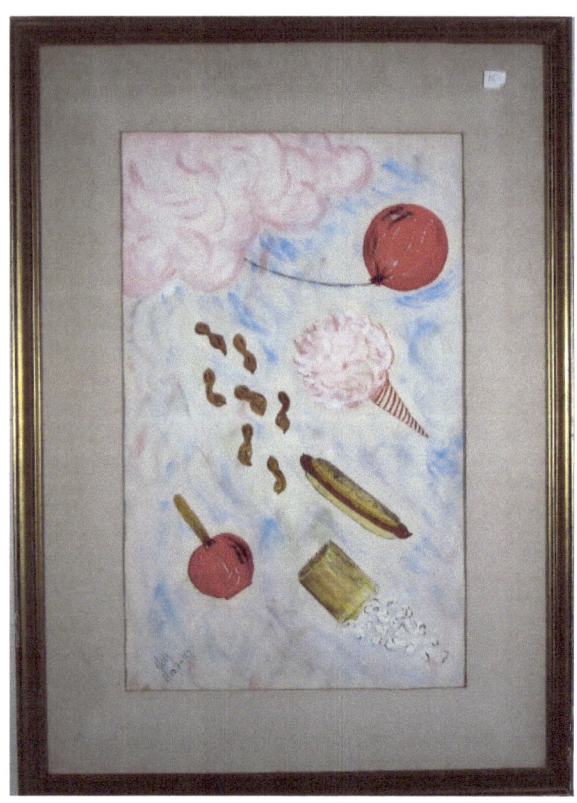

"State Fair Cravings"
Jay Jerkhoffer, 1957
Watercolor and body fluids on paper

Thought by some to be nothing more than a poor child's food fantasy, this art critic senses something far more primordial on display here. In this painfully honest disclosure of sexual frustration and missed opportunities, the discriminating art viewer sees nothing less than a symbolic representation of biblical "spilled seed". The artist Jerkhoffer has placed wiggling, tumbling spermatozoa and a deliciously phallic hot dog close to, but clearly missing the round, pink and red symbols of female voluptuous desire… In 1957, a young man in tight pants wandered throughout a noisy state fair working himself into a frenzy.

K.L.

"Why Fight For Freedom When You Can Vomit It?"
Xerxes Flannigan, 2002
Oil on canvas

This is another mystery painting whose meaning is left up to those masochists with enough patience to try to figure it out. Is the blind demon child projectile vomiting freedom or is the emotionless face with the "children of the corn" eyes revealing how the artist felt about him/herself? We'll never know. The unfinished quality of the work suggests that maybe it was just time to smoke some weed, eat a peanut butter and jelly sandwich and watch Star Trek reruns, because, "shit man, I've put enough time into this bullshit homework assignment." This is a masterpiece of combined self-indulgent teenage angst and boredom.

K.L.

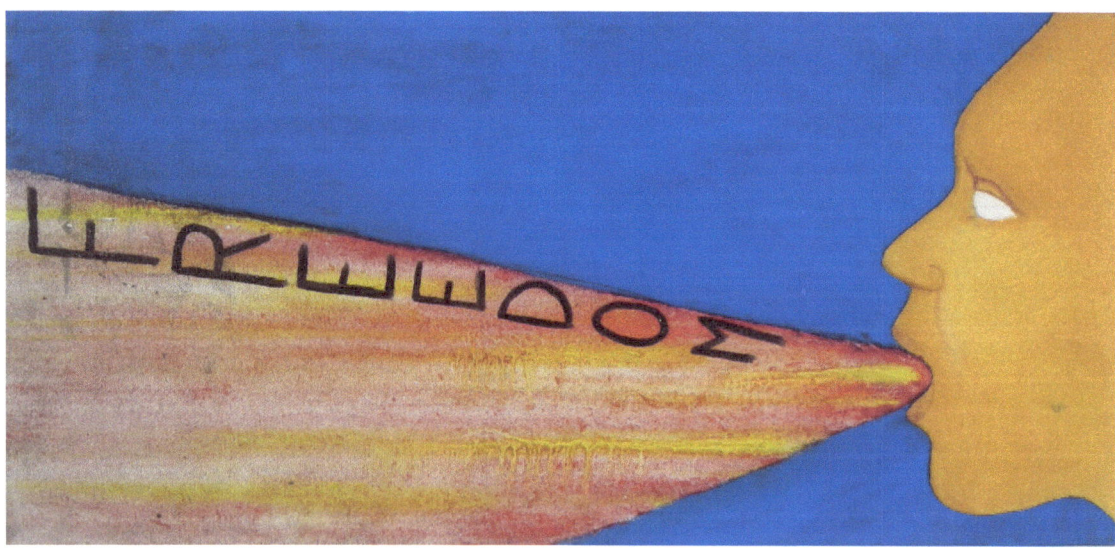

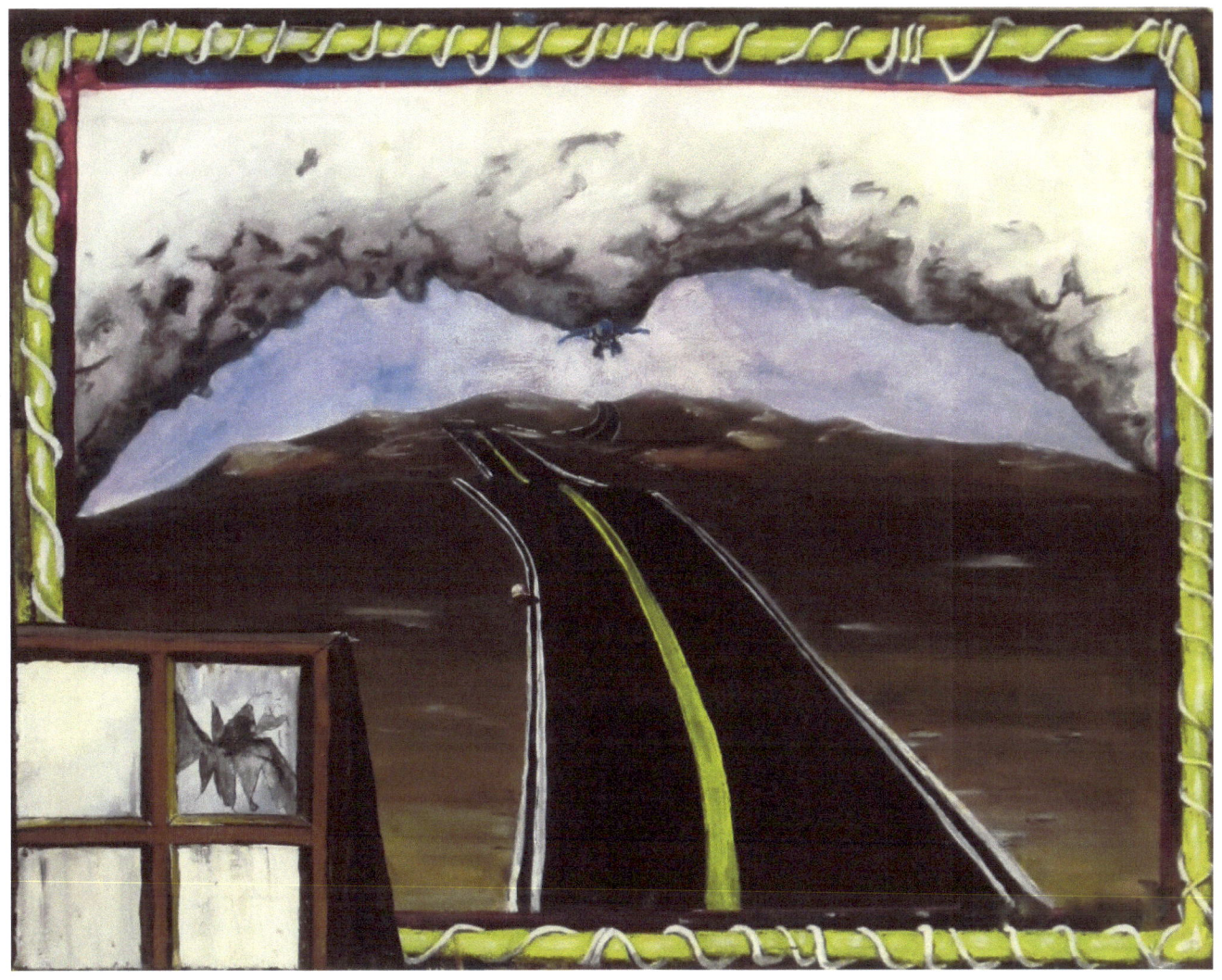

"Itty Bitty Blue Man's Weltanschauung"
Blanco Sauvage-Blanca, Transpersonal Ignoramic Glamification PhD., 1993
Oil on canvas

This work is just one in a profoundly thoughtful series by the artist Sauvage-Blanca. All of them merge the dynamic and often polar worlds of mansicular granulation and flaccid truspifaction while exploring the abstract idea of a cerebrally generated cosmos versus a materialistic crepuscular croprastitution. In this painting, we see a fractured glassive pane (the cosmic aperture) presumably leading to the macadamization of a geological terrazone that travels from near to far as observed by a miniature blue clad body whose dorsal and volar surfaces are stabilized by a stolagtitic victor vector. If we are befuddled by this desolate manscape, we should be; for its true meaning is far, far beneath most of us mere mortals.

K.L.

"You may be disappointed if you fail, but you are doomed if you don't try."
- Beverly Sills

"L'hippopotame Dansant"
Guillaume Apollinaire, 1917
Oil on canvas

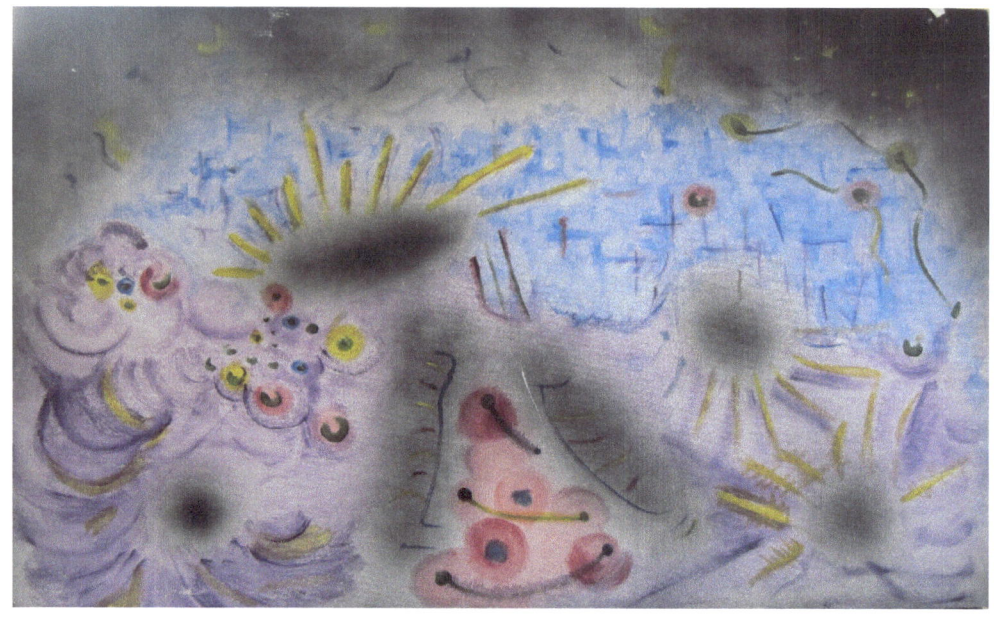

Our "people in the know" say that this extraordinary painting was part of the set decoration of the famous 1917 surrealist play "Les Mamelles de Tiresias" by Guillaume Apollinaire. It gave rise to the famous hippo mothballs craze that swept the Parisian art world in 1926. The dancing hippo represents the unconscious mind, which longs to be smothered in mothballs. They give off a radiant glow and offer enlightenment. The hippo is not under attack, but welcomes the invigorating smell of naphthalene. But, beware of the pyramid of red things at the bottom of the painting. They represent obstacles that block the inner mind's upward spiral. This painting is a stunning achievement in "le movement de hippo et boule de naphthlene."

Helmut Tuttass, PhD

"Portrait of Auntie Johansen"
Francis Fairchild, 1980
Oil on triple SSS board

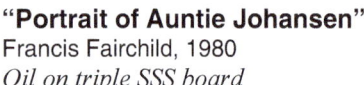

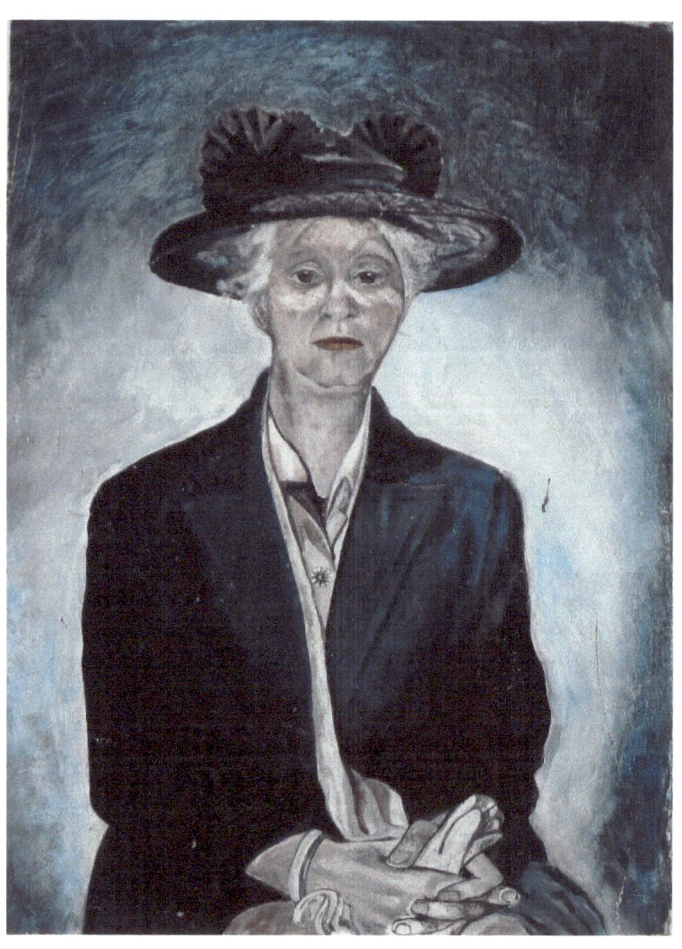

Looks are deceiving. Meet Auntie Johansen, parish priest caretaker, organizer of bingo night, ice cream socials and Saturday catechism lessons – a kind and quiet woman. In her younger days, as Colastie Solange, she was Louisiana's premier lady gator wrestler followed by an exciting stretch as Señora Montego, gunrunner for Che Guevara and then Hoosie Whatsis, a celebrated stripper in L.A.'s Thai Town. Behind those guarded eyes lies a world of secret identities and intrigue.

K.L.

"Bach's Universe"
Testy McTesterson, 2000
Acrylic on Canvas

"Sometimes, I sit alone under the stars and think of the galaxies inside my heart, and truly wonder if anyone will ever want to make sense of all that I am."

Testy McTesterson

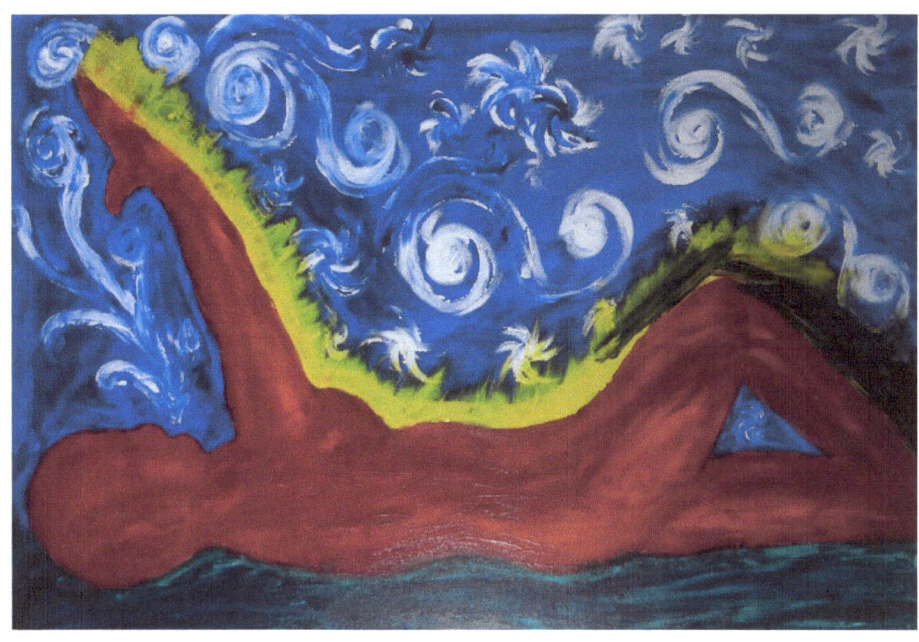

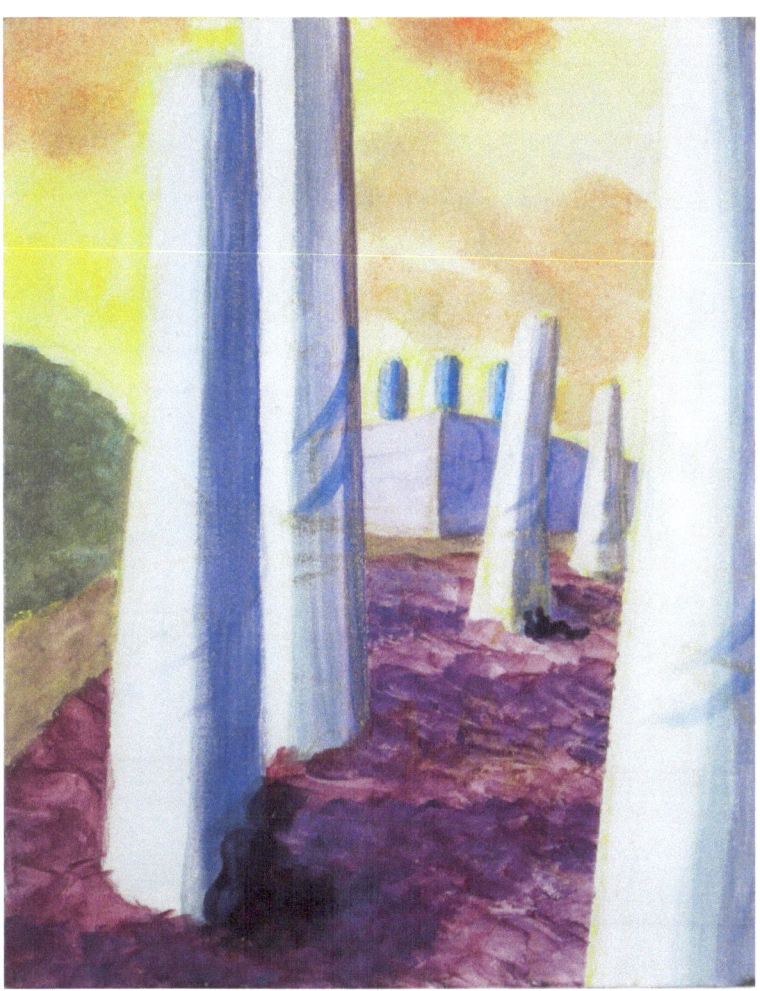

"All art is autobiographical. The pearl is the oyster's autobiography."
- Federico Fellini

"It's Never Too Late"
Sister Augusta Mimsey, 2016
Third-rate pigments mixed with Big Bird's uropygial gland secretions on canvas

A lifetime of repressed sexual desire is explored in this work of resigned loneliness and hopeless voyeurism. In a painting replete with phalli of many sizes and shapes the viewer senses the desperate intensity of a withered old nun's piercing gaze. Leaving the convent upon retirement, and after having first visited the adult novelty boutique, the old girl's next stop was the local lovers' lane where she indulged in some hardcore titillation. Then it was on to the candy store to buy chocolate, lots of chocolate. We eagerly look forward to more artistic explorations from the sensual powder keg that is Sister Mimsey.

K.L.

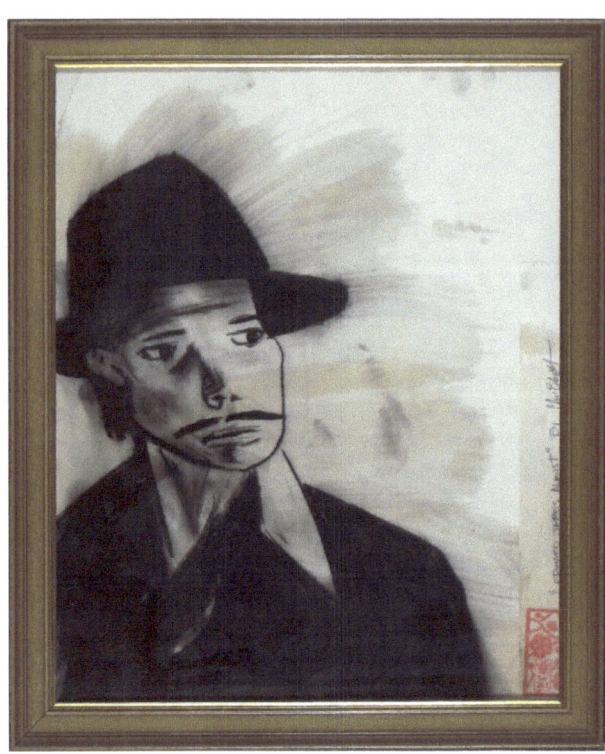

"Edward James Almost"
Cliv Blatly, 1981
Compressed charcoal and spilled Starbuck's Frappuccino on paper

The actor Edward James Olmos, on the set of the 1981 movie "Zoot Suit", has misplaced his lower jaw and anxiously struggles with his lines.

K.L.

"Geronimo Questions Reality"
George Larter, 2008
Acrylic, tears and mud on buffalo hide

George Larter's depiction of America's most famous Native American is truly one of his finest masterpieces. The quizzical inclination of the old man's head seems to ask, "Just what the fuck happened and how could it have ever gone so wrong?" His freshly washed and styled hair and neatly folded headband indicates a desperate attempt to embrace western society. Or are we witnessing a freeze frame of the old warrior a split second before his head is removed from his torso by a sneaky black bear? The fathomless gaze of the eyeless sockets approach perilously close to hypnotizing the viewer as they peer from within a landscape deeply etched from the pain of White Man's transgressions. This powerful piece simply oozes guilt ridden liberal empathy!

K.L.

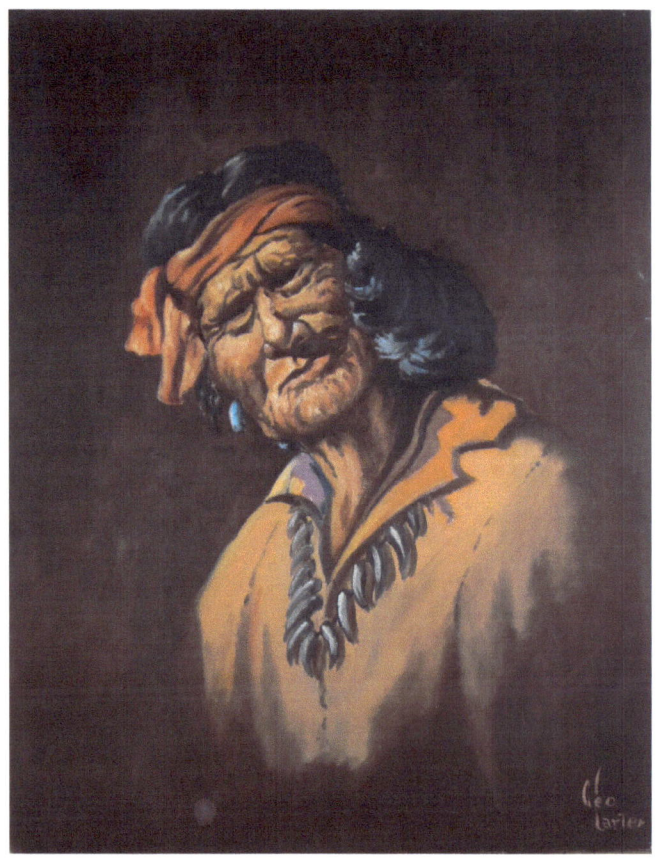

"Red Riding Hood, Rewritten"
C. lupus, 2002
Oil on canvas

Red, a member of PETA, meets the wolf, thinly disguised as Jed Clampett in his short overalls. Using the secret sign, he whistles to Comrade Red, guiding her to his secret cell in the forest where they will conspire to escalate deadly counter attacks in an effort to prevent future wolf pogroms. Castle Palin looms in the background; the bridgeless, glacial stream portends nothing but doom.

K.L. and J.O.

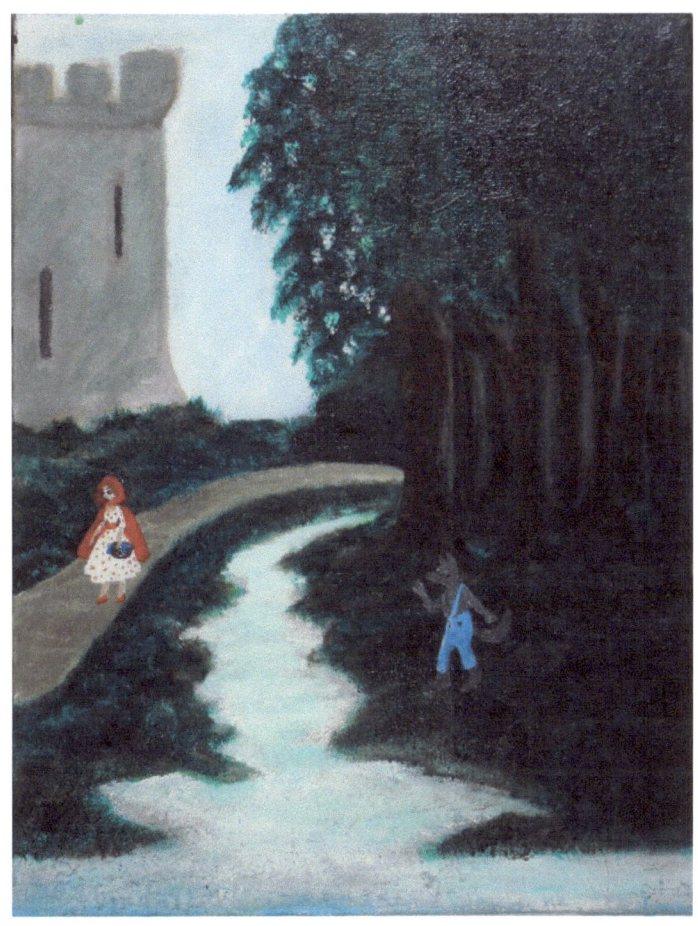

"Acceptance, under someone else's terms, is worse than rejection."
- Mary Cassatt

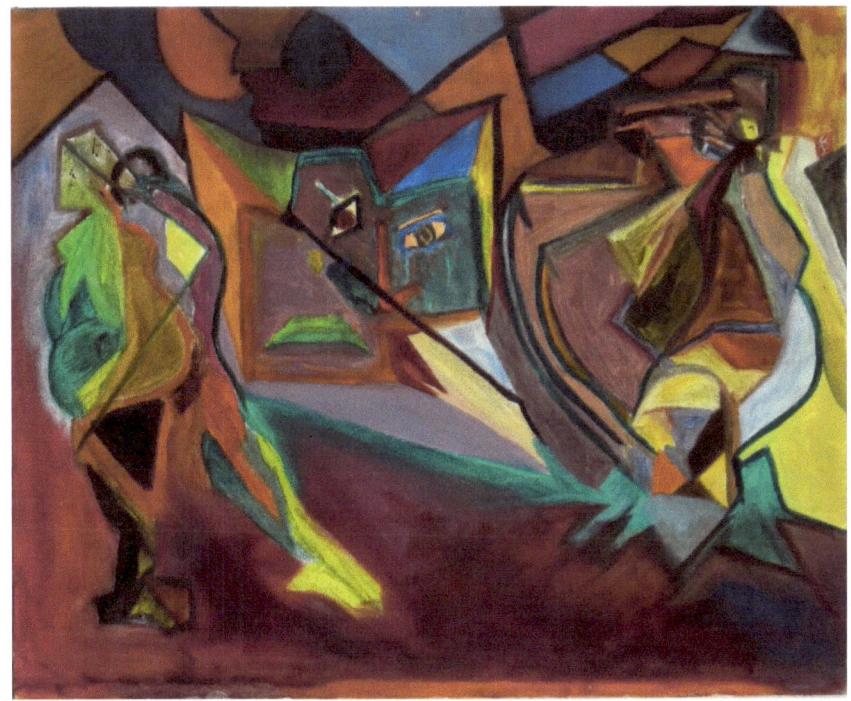

"Lance's Limbo Lingam"
Homerze Hardlithair, 1998
Oil on canvas panel

She showed him a shapely leg and her new yellow shoe and all he could do was hold his breath and swell up like a stained glass frog. Amused, others observed him from the sidelines gripping his face in anguished embarrassment and preparing for the imminent gut-spewing explosion. Suddenly from his unzipped pants sprang a rigid 5-foot black pole. Limbo dance music blasted from the p.a. system and his humiliation was complete.

K.L.

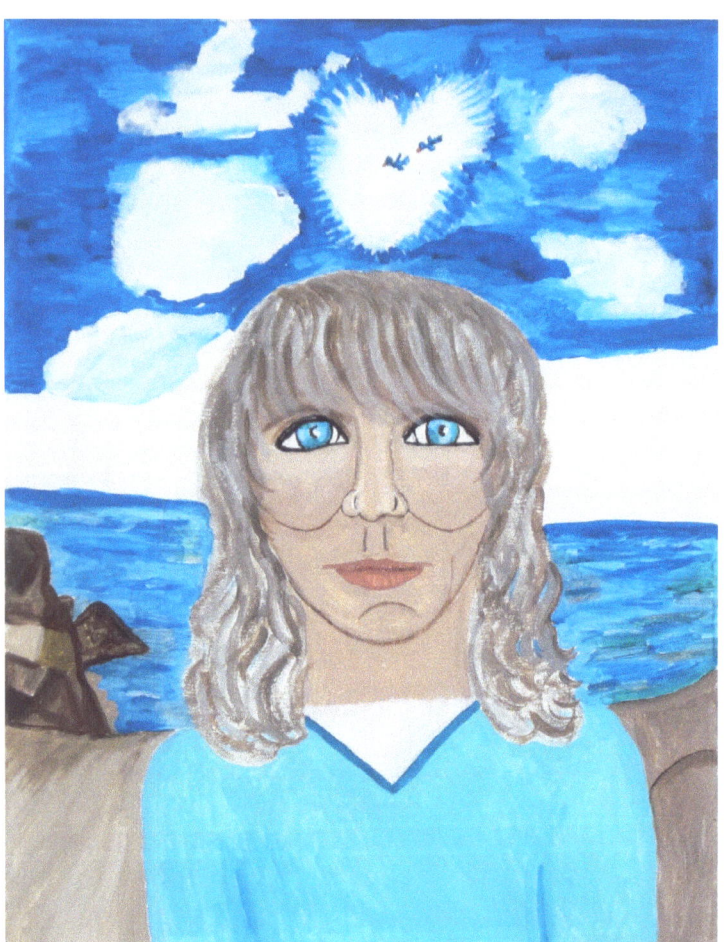

"The Blueness of it All"
Lordoma "Lordy" Lampkins, 2008
Acrylic on canvas

In this homage to summer romance, Lampkins adorns the object of his affection with Cocker Spaniel tresses and blue…lots of blue. His lovely Nordic lass, on vacation in a warm, tropical paradise, is dressed like she's in Stockholm on a winter's day and crowned by a cranium that would embarrass an Australopithecus. But, blinded by love, Lordy is oblivious to this, as well as her facial scars and vacant stare, indicative of recent cheek augmentation surgery and a prefrontal lobotomy. The fluffy heart cloud with flying birdies arouses our warm fuzzies while the blurry transport plane conjures cargo cults.

K.L. and J.O.

"Hoc Nefas Est"
Jonathan Ninnyhammer, 1975
Housepaint and tarpaper on canvas

The most significant thing about this piece is the enthusiastic response it generates whenever it is seen in public. The viewer is helplessly drawn into its multiplicity of shapes: the demolition of the Berlin wall, Mao Zedong leading the Long March, a profile of Vladimir Putin smoking a Meerschaum pipe, and Katherine Hepburn riding a bicycle through Central Park. As a turning point in his stuttering career this work allowed Ninnyhammer to consider transitioning into imagining and talking about, but never actually doing, the "Where's Waldo?" puzzles as well as large format tar paper collages which could have adorned the walls of roofing company offices nationwide.

K.L.

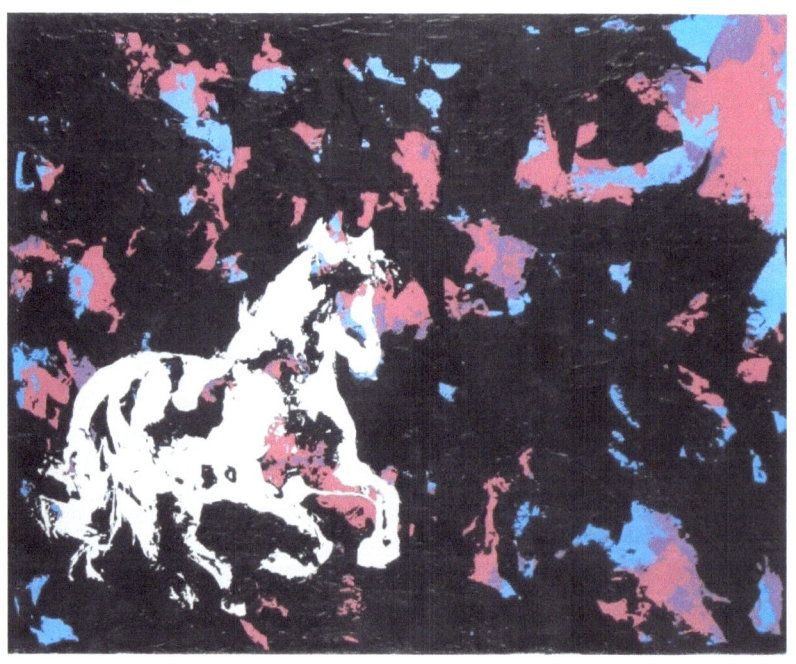

"Aquarium Turf War"
Mike Nelson, 1961
Mashed power bait, peanut butter, and Nutella on canvas

This intimate view of an ecosystem in crisis is captured by the retired scuba diver/artist/aquariumologist Mike Nelson. In a phenomenon never before seen by human eyes Nelson shows us a sinister bid, by a herd of pregnant sea monkeys, to take over the world one aquarium at a time. They have arrived en masse, nearly bursting with millions of nauplius larvae to expel into their newly purloined province. The entrenched coral overlords respond to the challenge with rigidly alert posture as they prepare to defend their watery realm. Since leaving "Sea Hunt" and the bright lights of Hollywood behind, Nelson has made moves into the art world with his unique niche creations dedicated to fighting underwater aquarium crime.

K.L.

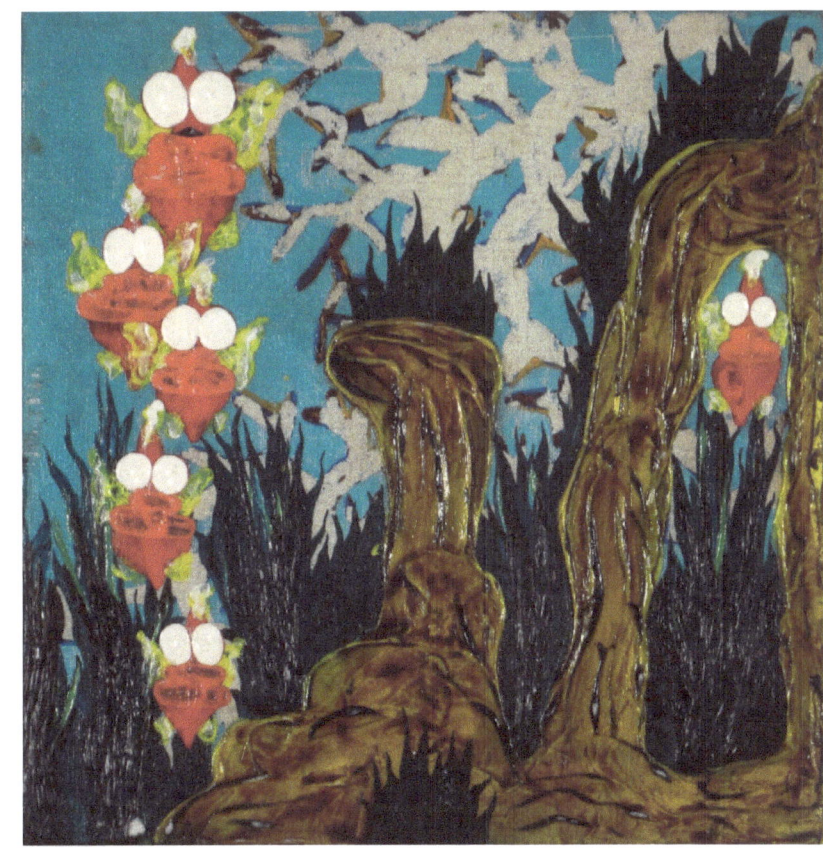

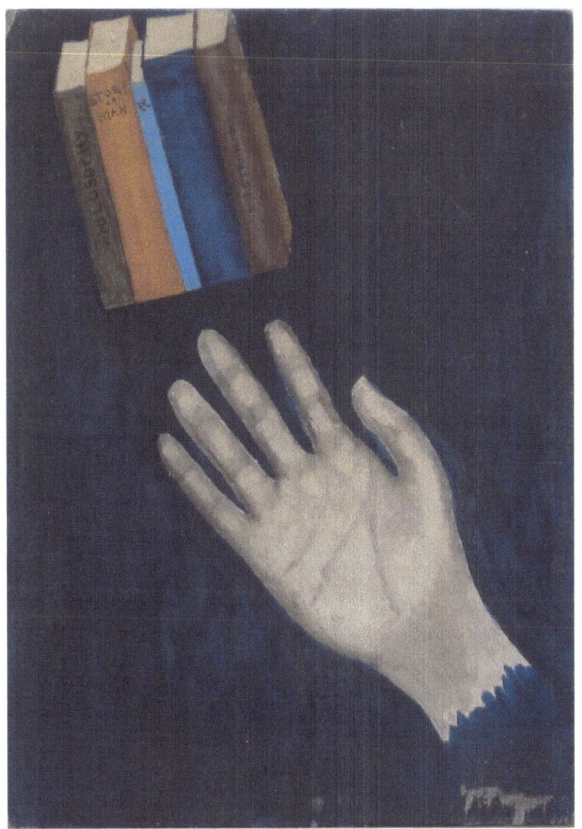

"How About a Big Hand for Those Books!"
Anonymous Bosch, 1970
Acrylic on Board

The Surrealist painter Bosch shows us, with the prophetic power of the subconscious mind, an obsessive, unrelenting search that would plague the artist his entire life - always striving, coming close, but never attaining a godlike perfect knowledge of all things. The disembodied hand with an open empty palm, oozes blue blood, (certainly referring to his fascination with horseshoe crabs) and symbolizes the detachment and sacrifice that all great intellectuals must endure to become the "knower of all things." Just as his fellow intellectual, Donald Rumsfeld knew, Bosch also knew that there are known knowns and known unknowns, as well as exactly 27 unknown unknowns still remaining. Since its unveiling, this painting has sparked lively reoccurring debates in surrealist art and philosophy circles concerning the contradiction between wanting to know more shit and actually being able to remember all that shit once you know it.

K.L. and J.C.

"Pinkness / Vagina Journey"
Deborah Doright 1968
Oil on canvas

Having finished her exhaustive study of the Dallas
Cowboys, this expressionist artist turned her
attention to inner healing. In this signature work by
Doright, most lovers of great art believe she has
unquestionably outdone herself. A vortex of spiritual
energy pulls us into the spontaneous synergism that
exists between the artist's oblique allusions to her
most deeply held equitable sublimations and the
four tightly structured edges of the canvas. With its
pure pink complexity Doright has carefully cultivated
a visual aesthetic intimately linked to a sense of
urgent "nowness" while simultaneously defying all
allegorical exegesis placed in her stony path or
foamy wake. The works "Armpitarama" and "The
Stuff Between My Toes" were created concurrently
with this work, all three representing a decade long
body-obsessive phase.

K.L.

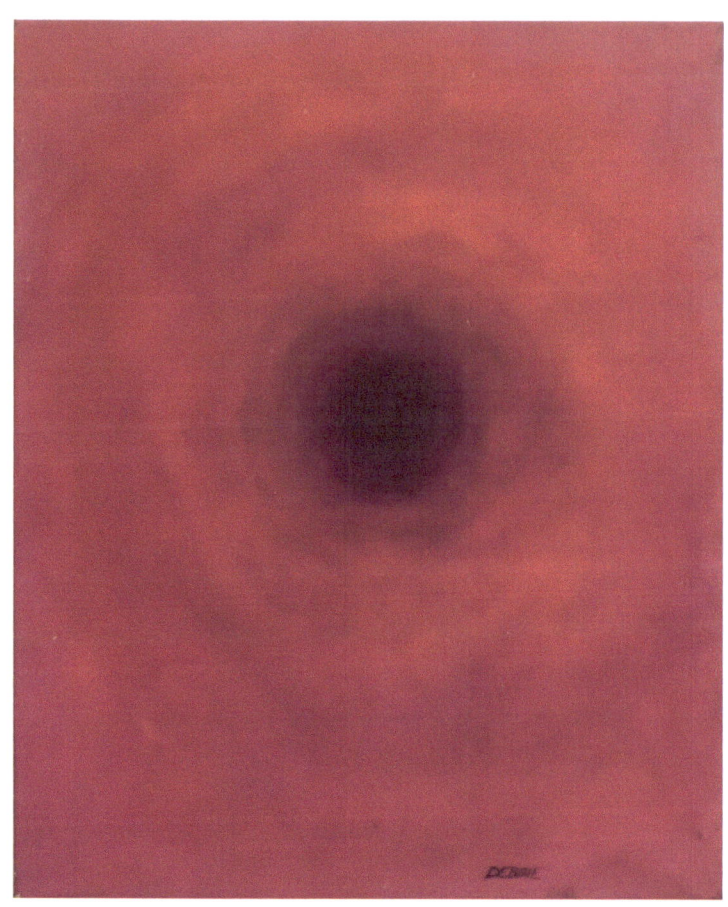

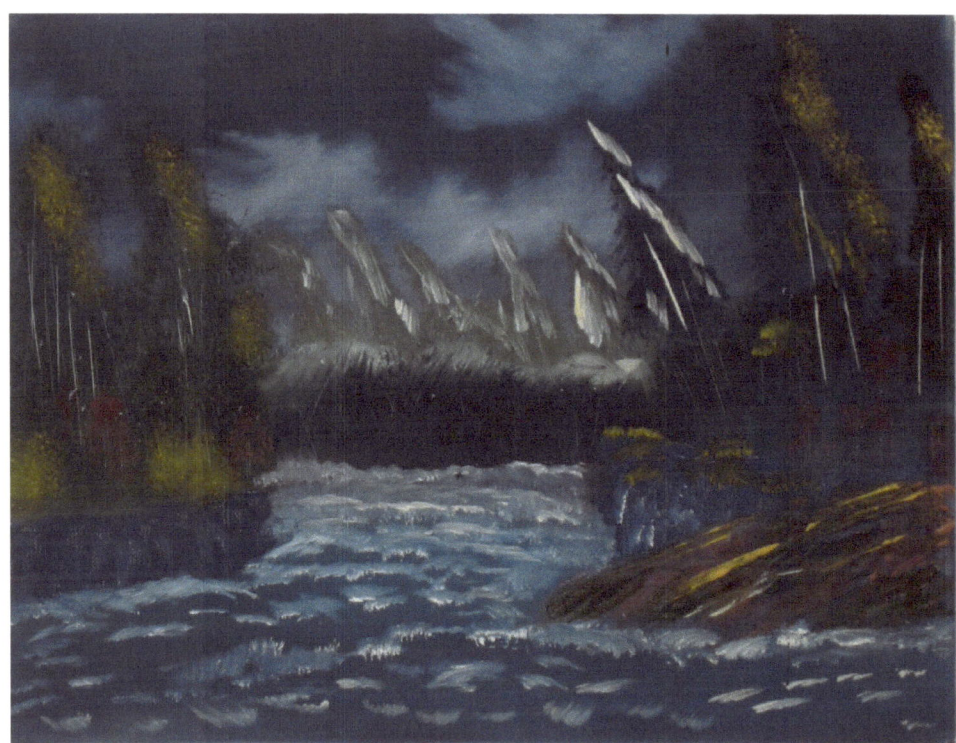

"Storm's a Comin' "
Artist unknown, 1980
Acrylic on board

Mt. St Helen has blown her
top. The energetic blast,
preceding the pyroclastic
surge, has arrived. Churning
and tossing, the river sweeps
forward to claim the artist and
her work. The forest is fucked.
The artist is fucked. Covered
with ash and mud, this tragic
record of the artist's final vision
was found face down in a
Tacoma KFC parking lot. This
landscape, as speed painting
at its best, gives new meaning
to "a la prima".

K.L.

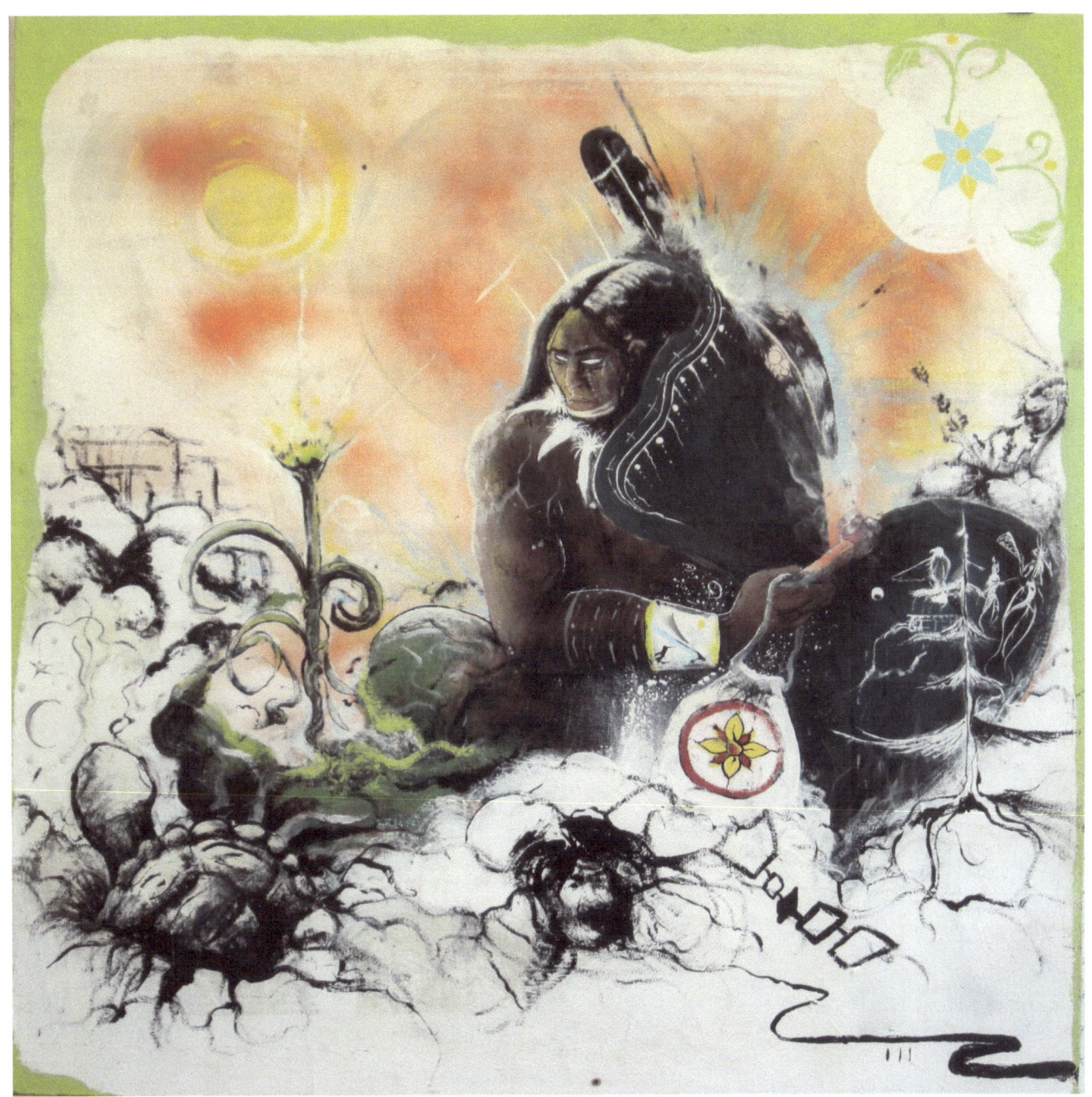

"Holy Man With Important Icons"
Bosco Nesitz, 2003
Acrylic on 14 pound plywood support with most excellent, recyclable eye hooks

Attracted to the solemn gravity of this work and feeling the magnetic pull of the shaman's white eyes, we dream about smoking the peace pipe and sharing his visionary powers. He exists in a place where emerging dirt turtles, pointing bald eagles in trees, floating legless fairies playing lacrosse, large Greek Quonset huts, giant stylized dandelions and shouting Old West pioneers live. We see all of this and we want to be there too. His blue glowing backpack is an entry port for the ultra high energy cosmic rays (aka UHECRs) he channels, which he then dispenses in Ziploc plastic bags on Wednesday afternoon between 2 and 4 behind the 7-11 at the north end of town to those born on the third Thursday of the month.

K.L.

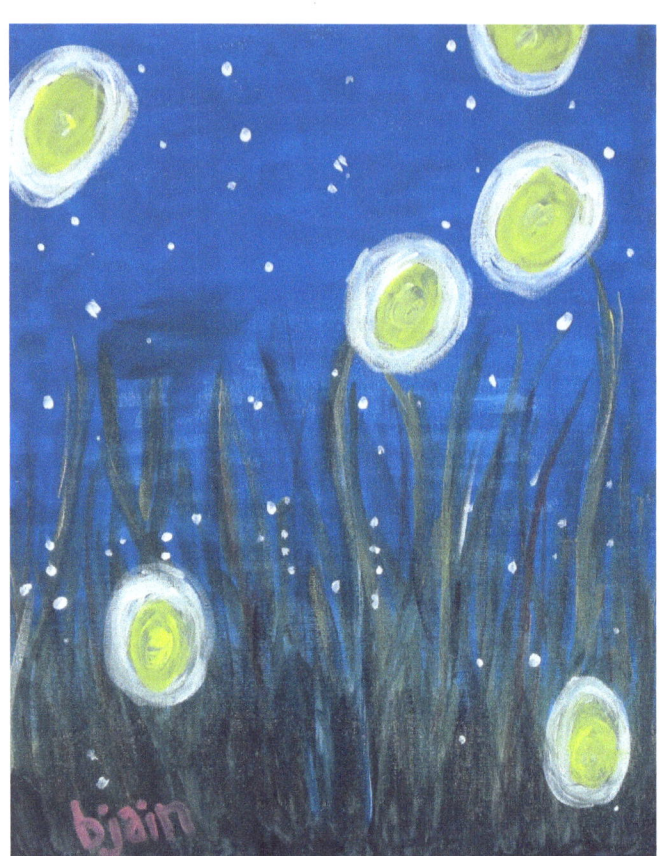

"Aunt Marge's Garden"
Ballin Jain, 1990
Acrylic on canvas

Breathe the night garden ether as the earth exhales beneath you. Earthworms slide by while crickets pulse and you submit, face down, in the cool grass. Are you lost in an entheogenic moment of a David Lynch movie or being pelted with Aunt Marge's deviled eggs drunkenly thrown at you from her back porch? When did she become such a sauce monster? Next time you certainly won't mention her rapid weight gain since the last time you saw her. Oh, wait… She just said she'd put you back in the will if you come over and cut the grass tomorrow.

K.L.

"An artist cannot speak about his art any more than a plant can discuss horticulture."
- Jean Cocteau

"Femsnake Killing The He/She"
Artist unknown, aprox. 2002
India ink on paper

Disturbing is all we can say about this one. It was lifted from the trashcan of an art therapy class at the women's' state penitentiary in Chowchilla California. Our team of consulting psychiatrists agrees that this artist suffers from the dreaded hugger-mugger syndrome characterized by suppressed rage and preoccupation with Andy Warhol fantasies. Murderous intent glares from the femsnake's left eye and the forked tongue threatens to give you a good lickin' if you get too close.

K.L.

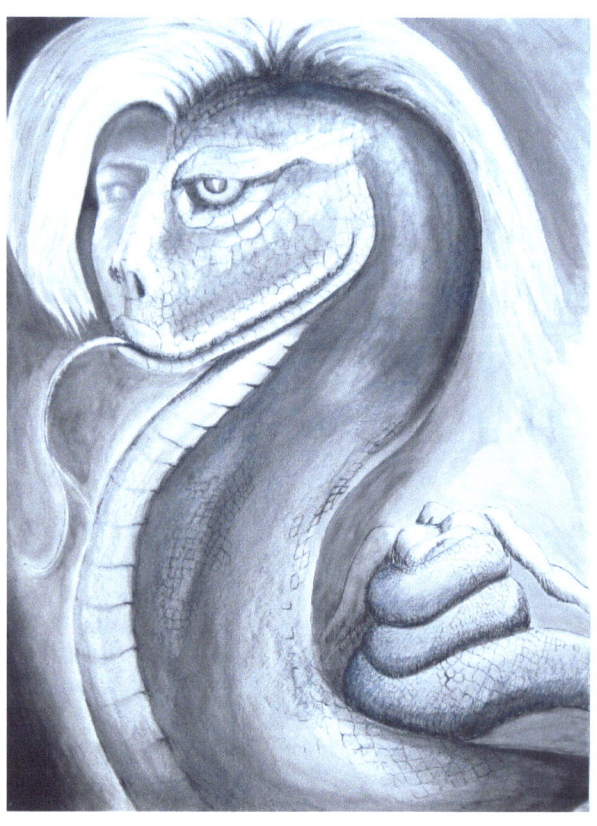

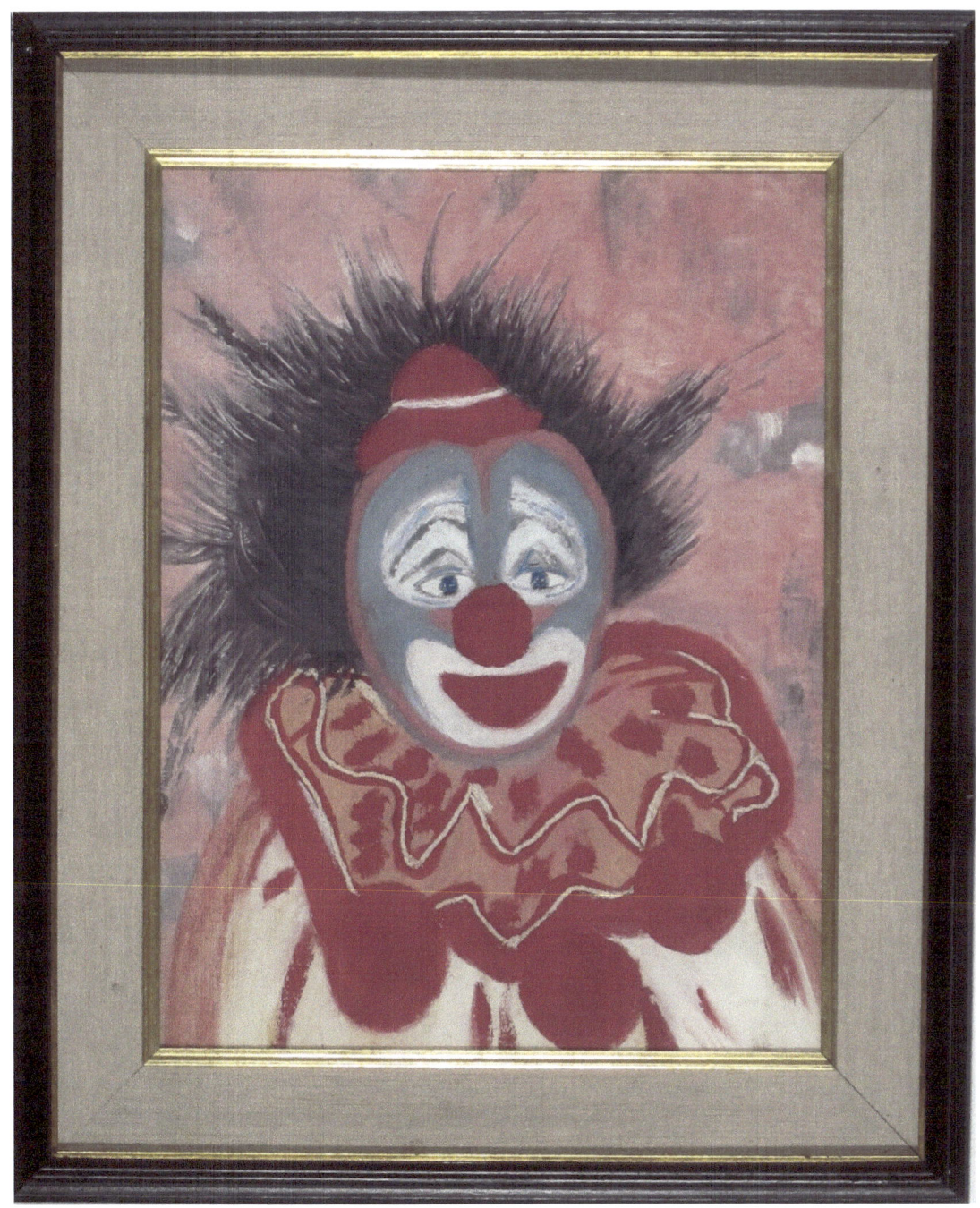

"Portrait of Bimbo the Elder"
Porky Chedwick, 1996
Oil on canvas board

It has been said:

"He will come amongst them as a childlike jester and some will open to his words as a flower to a bee. But most will laugh and ridicule him and drive him from their midst and be poorer for that. Know him then as your higher self to whom you refuse to give shelter and sustenance and know therefore that he wanders through this life a stranger to those he loves most. And when you see the one with vacant eyes, red nose and disheveled hair know that he cares not for the things of this world, but resides in a place that you will never know."

- Mama Ji

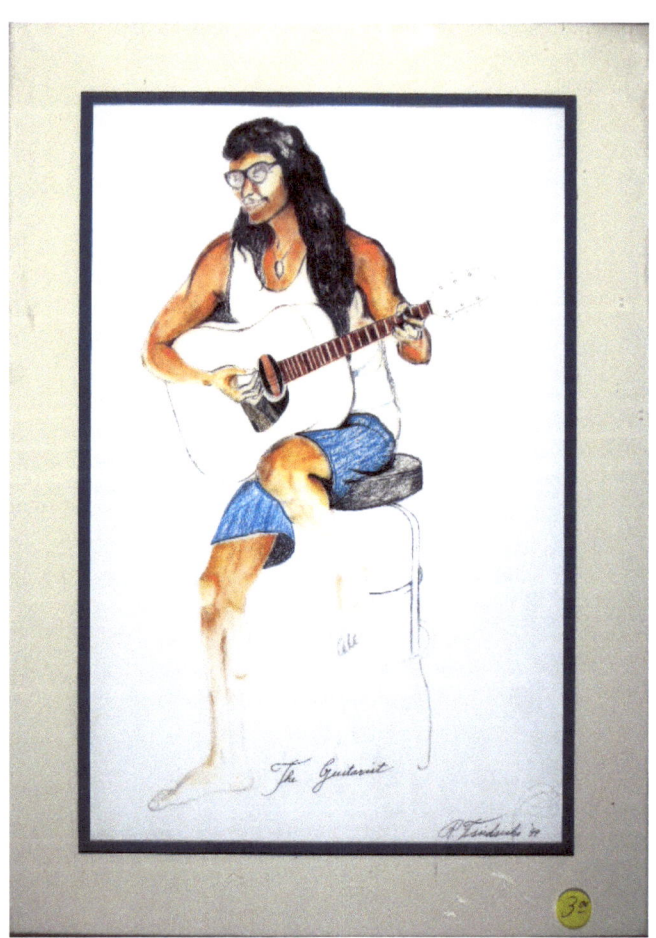

"The Guitarist"
Ritter Friedricks, 1999
Colored pencil on paper

This sensitively rendered portrait of Michael Jackson and "Weird Al" Yankovic's love child mysteriously turned up in a Jackson, California thrift store. In this quietly secluded foothill town, Friedricks, the "Artist For the Stars", maintains a studio where the portraits of many Hollywood love children adorn the walls. This elegantly understated work touchingly captures, despite his boneless right hand and balancing on a one legged stool, a talented young man's great determination to display the musical talents he has inherited from his world famous parents. The early stages of vitiligo and a laid-back So Cal fashion sense are proof positive of his lineage.

K.L.

*"Failure is the foundation of success...
success the lurking place of failure."*
- Lao Tzu

"Ripe Refuge"
Preston Puckerson , M.D. 2000
Oil on canvas

Salvaged from the dumpster of a Marin County proctology office that was being remodeled, this lovely piece was too yummy for us to pass up. The soft rendering of the plump juice sacs that circle the gaping aperture speak to us of a pliant acceptance and a quiet escape from a crazy world. The juxtaposing of the massive berry (the painting is 10'x10') and the ethereal blueness it floats in creates an undeniable tension on the canvas. We found the artist walking to and fro from the dumpster so we asked him to help us understand his extraordinary piece. Dr. Puckerson only sighed and said that the painting was responsible for collapsing the wall in his office as well as his 30-year marriage. "She was a very unyielding, retentive, woman! She hated my big fruity pictures," he said.

K.L.

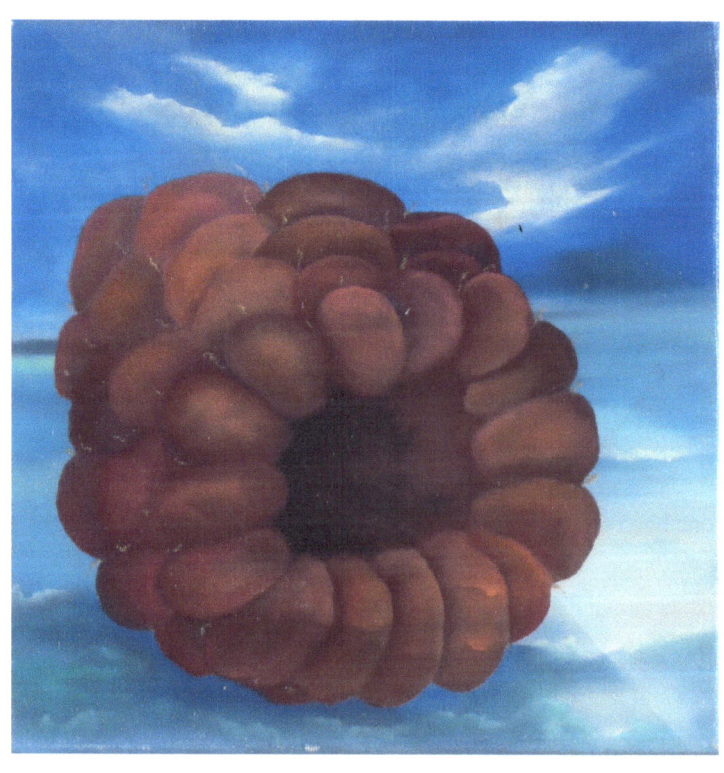

"Tequila Dreaming"
Frank Lloyd Wright, 1935
Acrylic, china marker and guacamole on velvetone Masonite

The great American architect Frank Lloyd Wright was known to have executed multiple painted mockups prior to creating prototypes for all his masterpieces. This highly symbolic mockup echoes Frank's oft politely overlooked misspent teen years south of the boarder in an Oaxacan jungle brothel. The high contrast china marker lines rebelliously strike out across the matt surface probing, pushing and thrusting as they explore the lush green Venus mounds. All this is accompanied by a generously languid flow of tequila tumbling over the rocks. It is thought that a pubescent fascination with Mexican fish ladders spawned the idea for his Pennsylvanian forest masterpiece. This unsigned and undated cryptic sketch reflects the artist's underlying insecurity about the design of so many unsupported cantilevered surfaces, which fly in the face of gravity-based Newtonian physics.

K.L. and J.O.

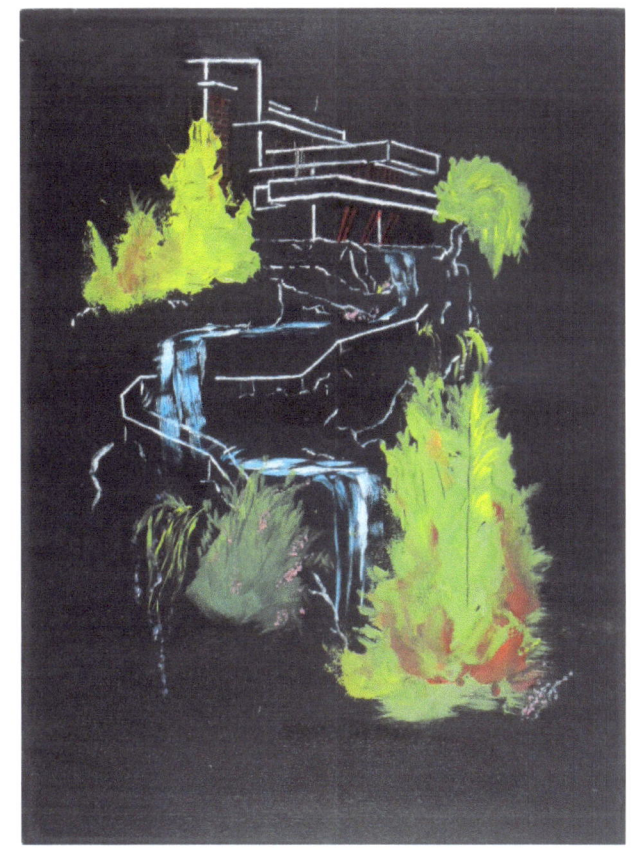

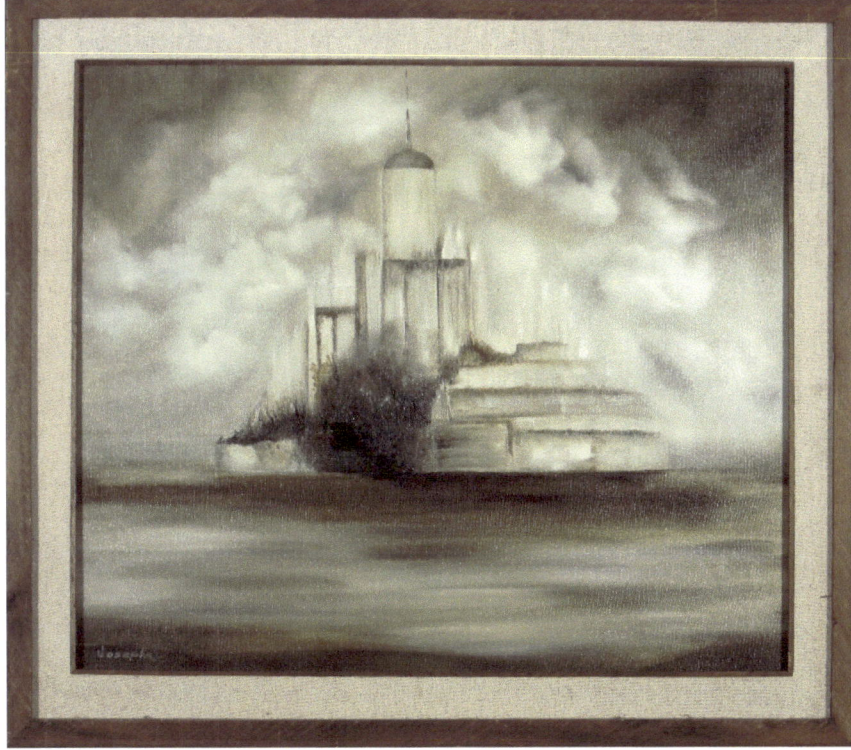

"Mississippi Come Up"
Josepha Josepha, 1970
Creek bottom mud, fermented bullfrog skins, crushed crawdad carapace on canvas

The artist/science fiction author Josepha depicts the phenomenon known as the caridoid escape reaction - CER. The reasons for this occurrence are shrouded in mystery and seeing it was a stroke of unusual luck. Josepha Josepha painted the CER from memory, as it had occurred 100 feet from shore in the Mississippi river. Storm clouds gathered as the islet threw itself up from the murky depths with algae dripping and crappies flapping. Josepha claims to have heard Richard Wagner's "Ride of the Valkyries" echo across the water as a giant showerhead descended from above and washed everything nice and clean.

K.L.

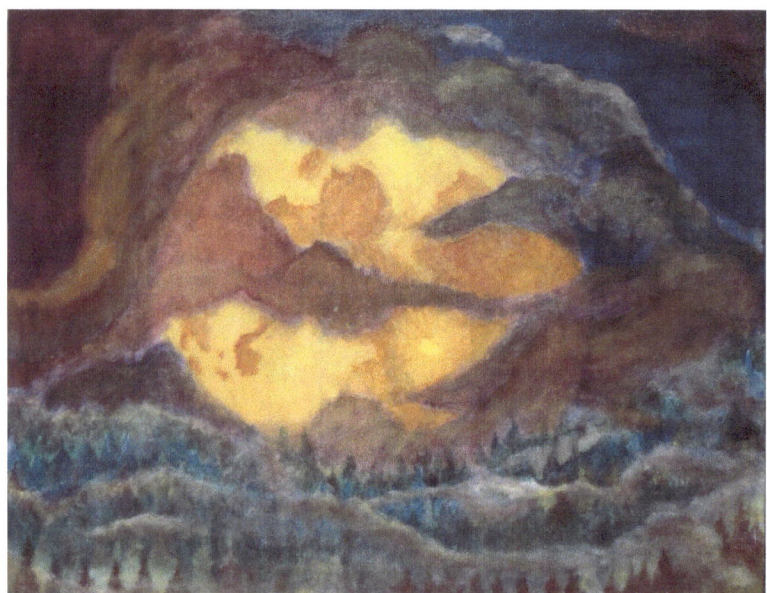

"In the Thick of It"
Kuné Jupon, 2010
Oil on canvas

The sound of two black holes colliding, massive gaseous ball, multitudinous cries of terror and despair…
The smell of bacon frying, realizing your survival backpack won't get you thru this one, all conflict is moot…
Were you a good person? Should have eaten the second piece of pie, hated less…
Alarm clock, just a dream, the sound of two black holes colliding…

K.L.

"Teetering on the Brink"
Nell Grover Kulb, 1890
Watercolor and colored pencil on paper

Highly valued by anthropologists and zoologists alike, this work may very well be the last image of the now extinct Oregon Legless Rockhopper. Arriving in the Pacific Northwest in the mid 19th century, this clan of transplanted Kentucky farmers was shunned by long legged folks who drove them into the most remote valleys where they quickly came into contact with the native Sasquatch population. Sadly, modern day field zoologists have, upon examining contents of the Sasquatch desiccated fecal pellets, found Rockhopper bones and hair remains. Based on these findings scientists have concluded that Rockhoppers were the main food source of the elusive wild hominids for at least 50 years. Not known for their symmetrical facial features or intelligence, this Rockhopper peers imploringly at the viewer, like a frightened cocker spaniel, clutching the sand with a skinny pink paw. Afraid of being swept downstream by the 2" torrent that surrounds her, she is apparently unaware of the hungry eyes that watch her from the dark forest behind.

K.L.

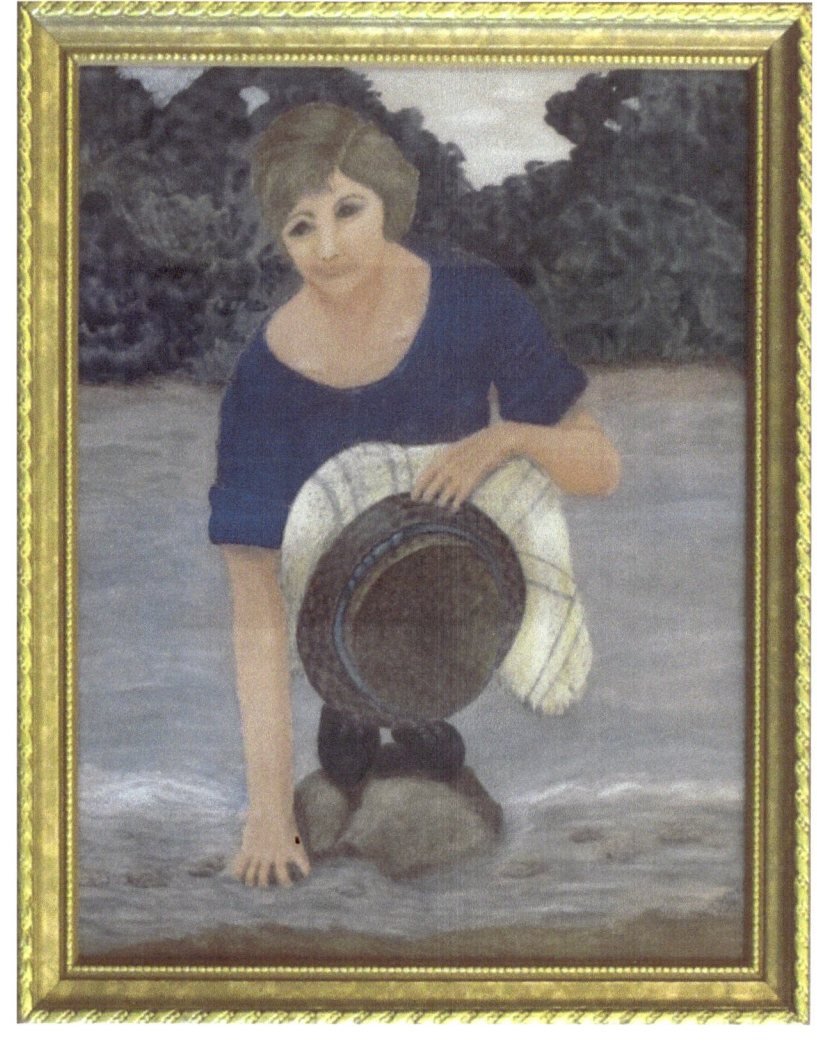

"Boys Will Be Boys"
Reginald Langford Helmhurst, Chief Chronicler of Manly Games, 1956-66
Acrylic on canvas

"High Cockalorum" aka "Polly on the Mop Stick," "Strong Horses Weak Donkeys," "Hunch Cuddy Hunch," "Finger Thumb and Rusty Bum," and "Jump the Knacker" was, in times past an English game that was popular among large groups of raucous young men. Once the champion of Birmingham's High Cockalorum club, this handsome frat boy at times had lots of fun playing hide and seek in a closet full of tutus. The artist Helmhurst captured the excited energy of the hunt with a singular intimacy and obvious advanced artistic skill.

K.L.

"The perfection of art is to conceal art."
- Quintilian

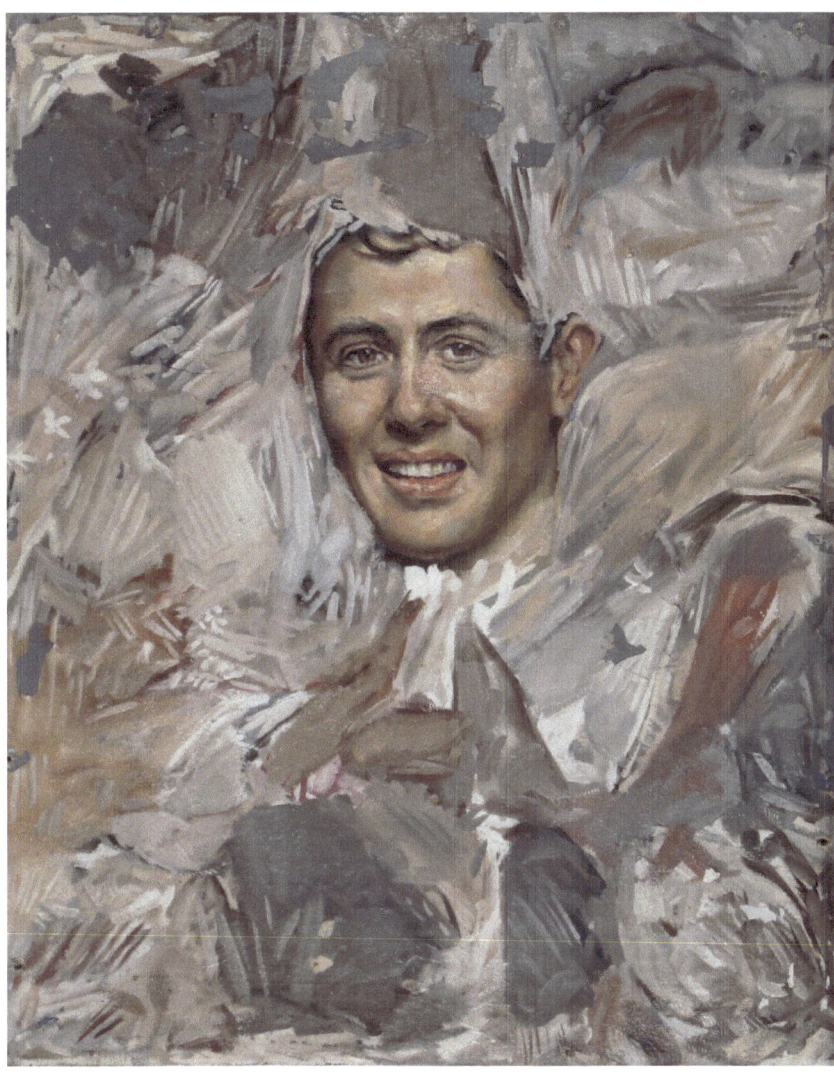

"Neanderthals In Hell"
Urgnuk Mugmoe, 1996
Campfire ash mixed with bone marrow and congealed carcass juice on slate

In a deep trance state the artist Mugmoe returns to the vision that invariably haunts him after dining on his favorite steak tartare. In the dream his Neanderthal tribe violently overwhelms a neighboring Homo sapiens clan. The battle is brief and brutish; screaming women and bundles of reindeer jerky are taken as well as a coveted Dark Souls III video game. In this painting the attackers' faces seem troubled – revealing that even human subspecies fear divine retribution and the consequences of not having wiped out all of the spear throwing, big browed geeks.

K.L.

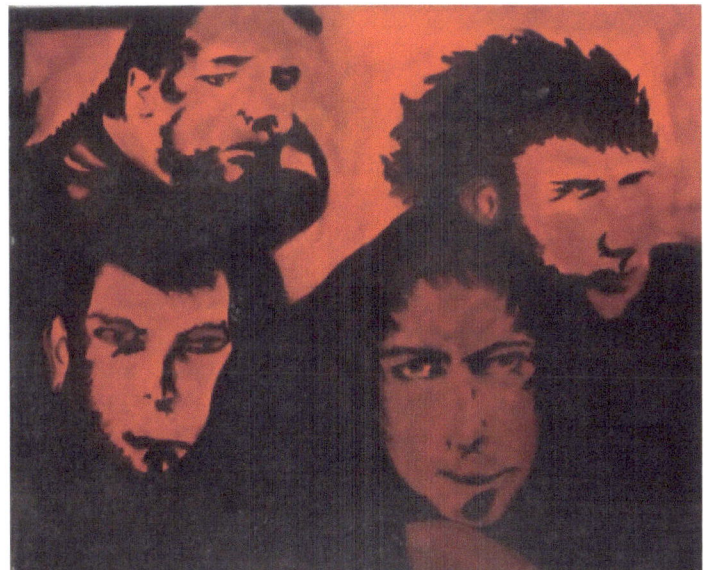

"Out Of the Void"
Elvis, 1979
Pen and ink, bourbon whiskey on paper

We thought he was dead too, but it appears since his "demise" in 1977 the King Of Rock and Roll has been living quietly in Petaluma California! Here, in an unassuming chicken coop, the music superstar has been channeling for an ancient Pomo shaman's ghost by creating drawings of unmatched sensitivity of a once prominent Native Californian tribe. Apparently the native man, being a fan of Harrison Ford movies and aware of Elvis' weakness for high fashion, requested that Elvis place a sassy little Indiana Jones hat on his head. We are thrilled that Elvis has nurtured this connection to the spirit world and you can bet that we will be keeping our eye out for more priceless gems from our Mississippi hip swiveler!

K.L.

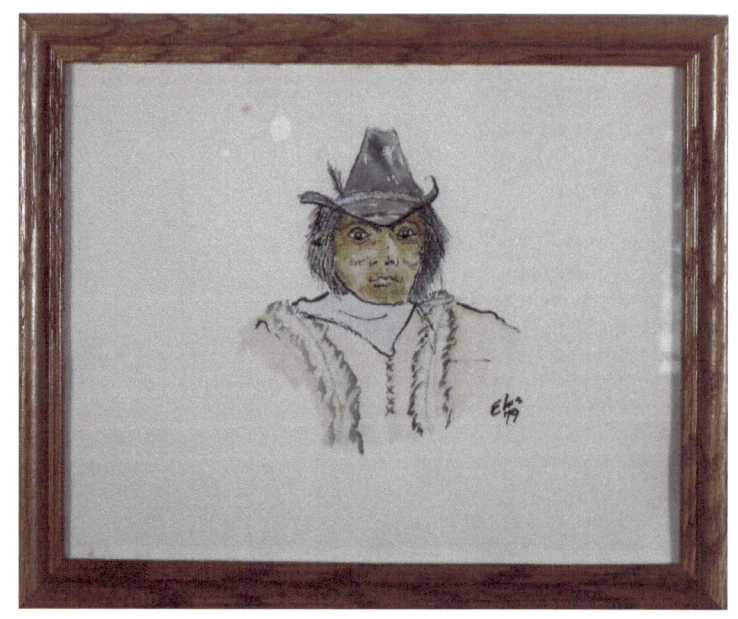

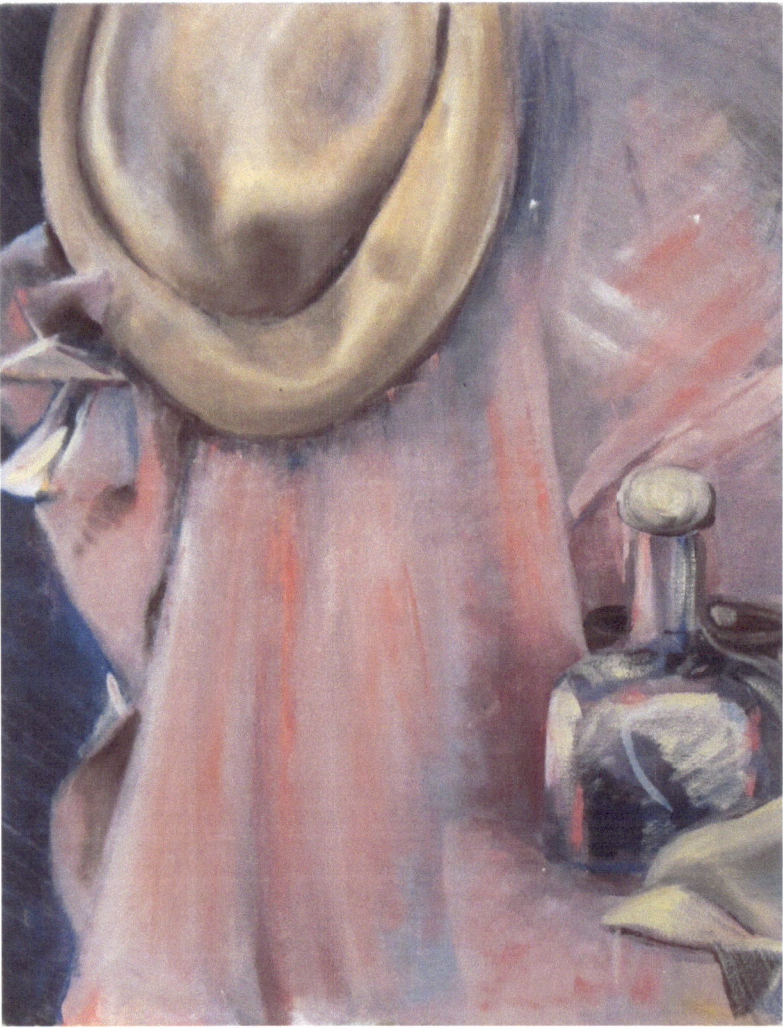

"When I am finishing a picture, I hold some God-made object up to it - a rock, a flower, the branch of a tree or my hand - as a final test. If the painting stands up beside a thing man cannot make, the painting is authentic. If there's a clash between the two, it's bad art."

- Marc Chagall

"Puddles and Jumbo Haiku"
Artist Unknown, 1983
Oils on artist canvas panel

Clown rides elephant.
See giant condom waiting.
Perfume will smell good.

K.L.

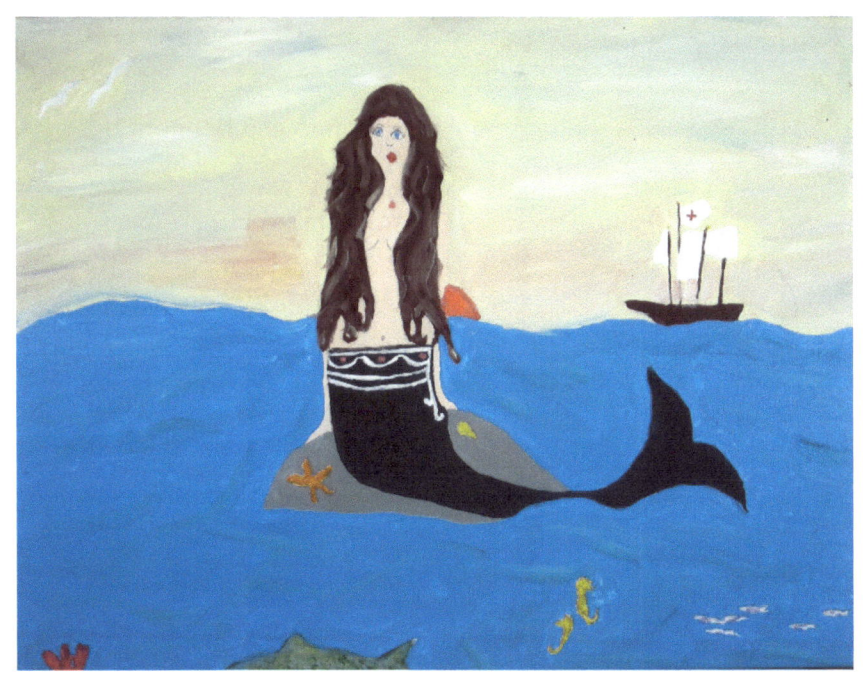

"Captain's Platter"
Arial Sushi, 1990
Acrylic on canvas

In this charming piece the well-known canned tuna label artist, Arial Sushi, ventures out of her market driven art rut to explore the budding sexuality of a fantastical Homo humpback. The pretty little mermaid's nether parts will be denied her eagerly approaching, sea hardened sailor, and the young siren seems in a confused quandary. The blue waters, littered with the floating bodies of other sea creatures, symbolize the many cast-off suitors who have yearned - to no avail - for her salty embrace.

K.L. and J.O.

"Creativity is allowing yourself to make mistakes. Art is knowing which ones to keep."
- Scott Adams

"Nasty Nancy"
Pony Boy Brown, 1985
Watercolor on paper

Dear Nancy,
Before you agree to a close up portrait, here are a few words of advice:
So that viewers can actually see your face, get a hair cut first; smile - don't sneer, it makes folks nervous; double chins multiply when you scrunch up your neck so wear a turtle neck and finally, if possible, try to think nice thoughts because even a pretty blue blouse doesn't disguise the calculating gaze of a mean lady.

Sincerely,
K.L.

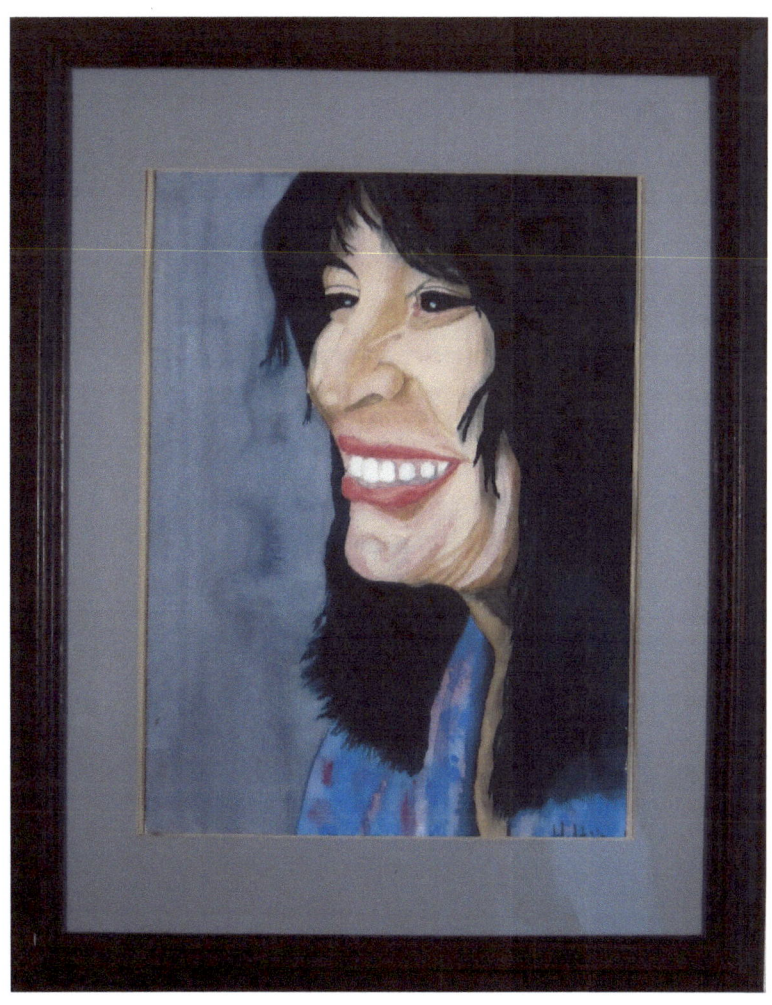

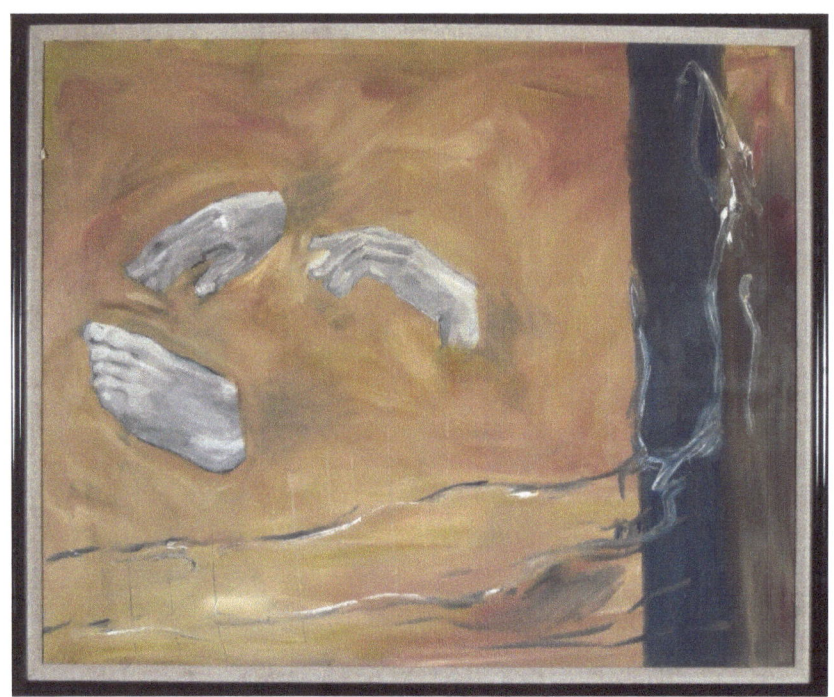

"Nilla Wafers and Nanners Next Time"
Netta Widdie, 1998
Acrylic on canvas

In this quietly desperate painting, the artist grapples with her life threatening butterscotch pudding obsession. Here she envisions herself going down for the count in a thick river of it. With only vicious barbed wire to grasp, she knows she couldn't get out if she tried. Flailing hands are now resigned to their fate; no one has rescued her so she'll just have to eat her way back to shore. A wooden fence post, symbolizes a father figure, as it watches with stiff, judgmental aloofness.

K.L.

"Cold Shower, No Eye Contact"
Sister Jill O'Sea, 2003
Watercolor and pencil on paper

This intimate portrait of Sister Mary Goodly and Father Fletcher captures a tender moment; after a Sunday afternoon bike ride in the company of parishioners, they are perspiring and flushed with their vigorous exercise. Halos interlinked like holy sprockets, but bodies held chastely apart, they surrender to a mind meld as they attempt to transmogrify their libidinous longings. Apparently they are successful, for they have become transparent as their Eros drains away, revealing their beating hearts of purest red still true to a higher calling.

K.L.

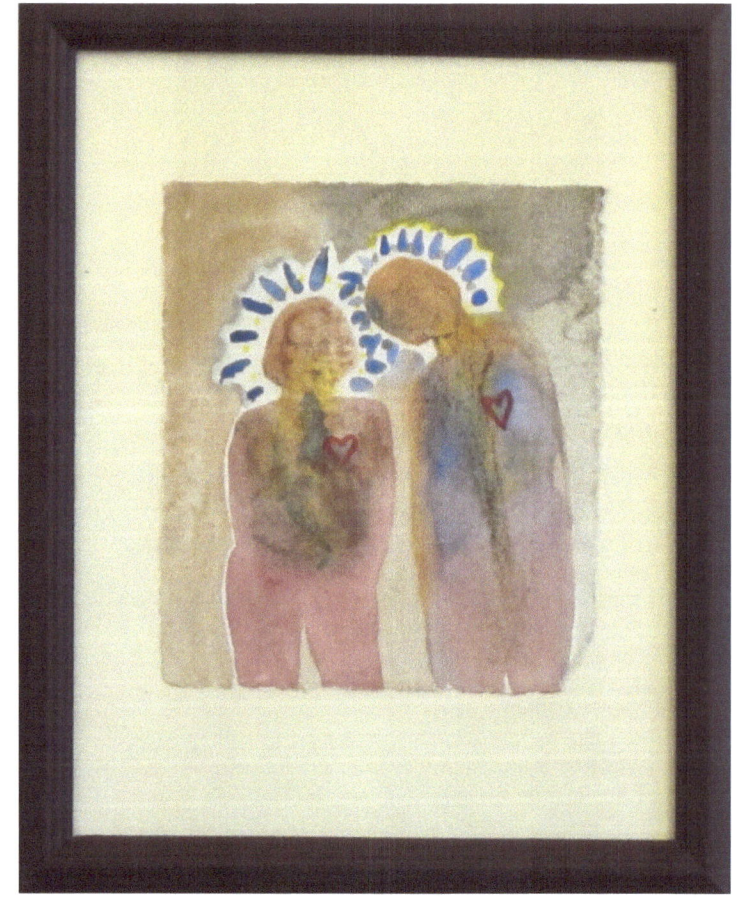

"Barbara's Bender"
Nelva Morningside, 1981
Acrylic on canvas board

Wearing a green rubber Hefty Bag, Barbara attempts a challenging new yoga pose.

J.O.

"The artist is nothing without the gift, but the gift is nothing without work."
- Emile Zola

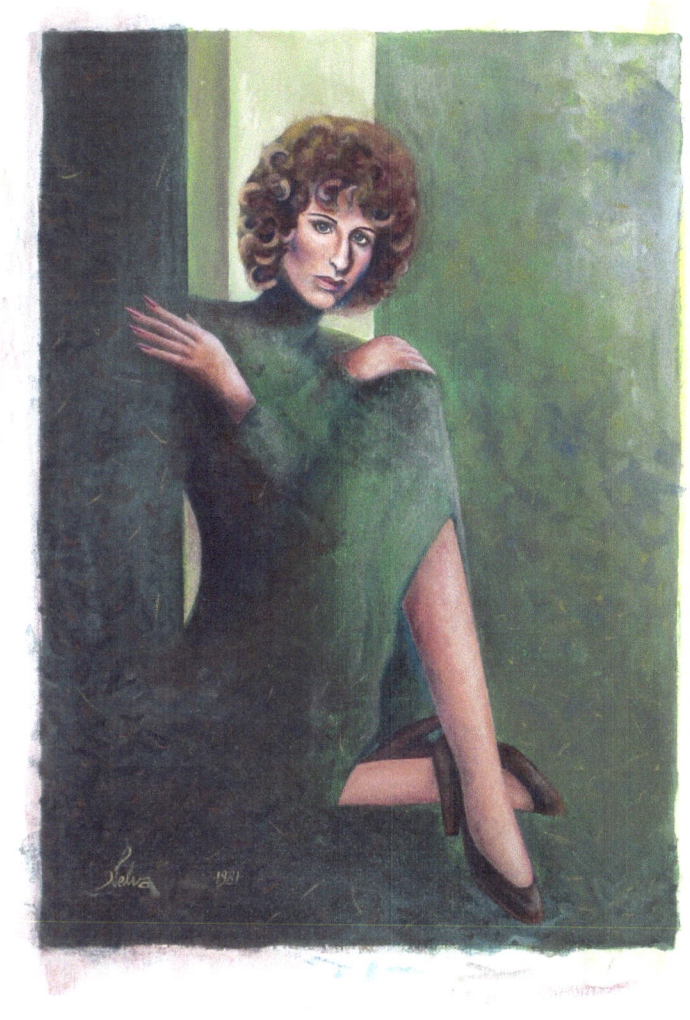

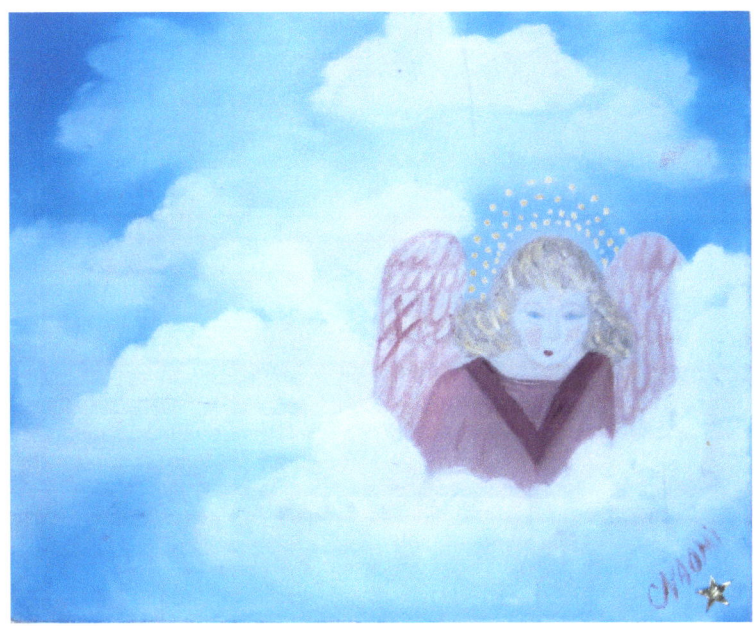

"Soft, Soft, So Soft"
Naomi Pupster 1966
Acrylic on canvas

Pupster revisits her most common narrative that springs from a reoccurring dream of angelic observations from on high. In this ever-so-soft and quiet piece – some might say vapid and pointless, she is alone in heaven and spying (never a good idea) down on her earthbound boyfriend; the pursed lips reveal a certain displeasure at her discovery. Actually, we had to dig deep to harvest some meaning from this insipid bit of pastel fluff. To be perfectly honest, the decently rendered clouds are the only reason we rescued this one. It has been honored with a gold star for being the most snoringly boring piece in the collection.

K.L.

47

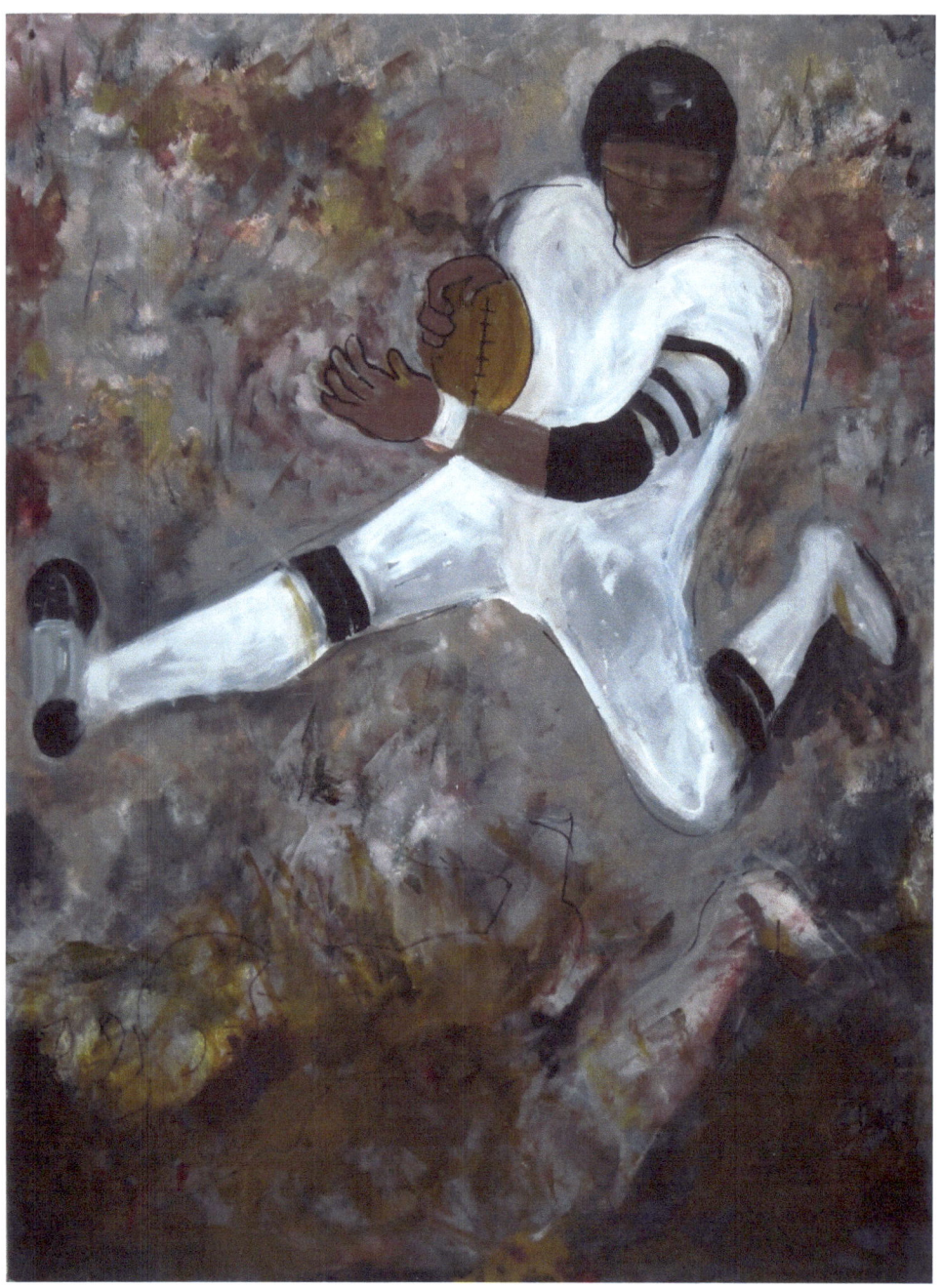

"Rough Men Like it Rough"
Herbut Slammer, 1989
Acrylic, black felt tip on Masonite

Inspired by the legendary Oakland Raiders football club, the gifted sports artist, Herbut Slammer, masterfully portrays the violent nature of a game played by bold, powerful men on a muddy gridiron in front of thousands of adoring fans. With impressionistic flair this timeless piece immerses us in the chaos of the moment as our hero, against a backdrop of suspended blood, mucous and vomit, leaps athletically over his vanquished opponents; Leading with his prosthetic right foot he narrowly misses what appears to be a roiling pool of feces and mangled body parts. The featureless face silently challenges us to consider the oppressive dichotomy of a grunting, struggling masculinity versus a righteous desire to soar above it all. It is ultimately the artist's boldness and uncompromising vision that takes this masterpiece down the field and into the end zone.

A.O.

"The Day After the Life Before"
Constance Fleeters, 1985
Watercolor on paper

Pink eye, booze and a ravenous gambling habit dwell heavily on this once lovely visage. Her direct gaze unabashedly challenges us not to be judgmental. But of course we are. No doubt she's been ridden hard and put away wet more than once; She probably deserves it…

K.L.

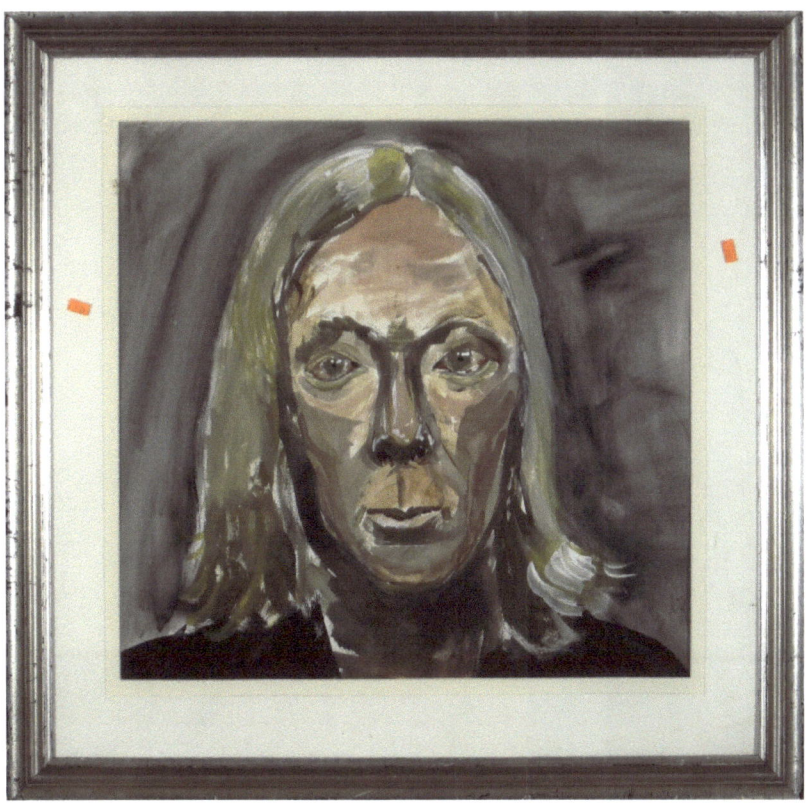

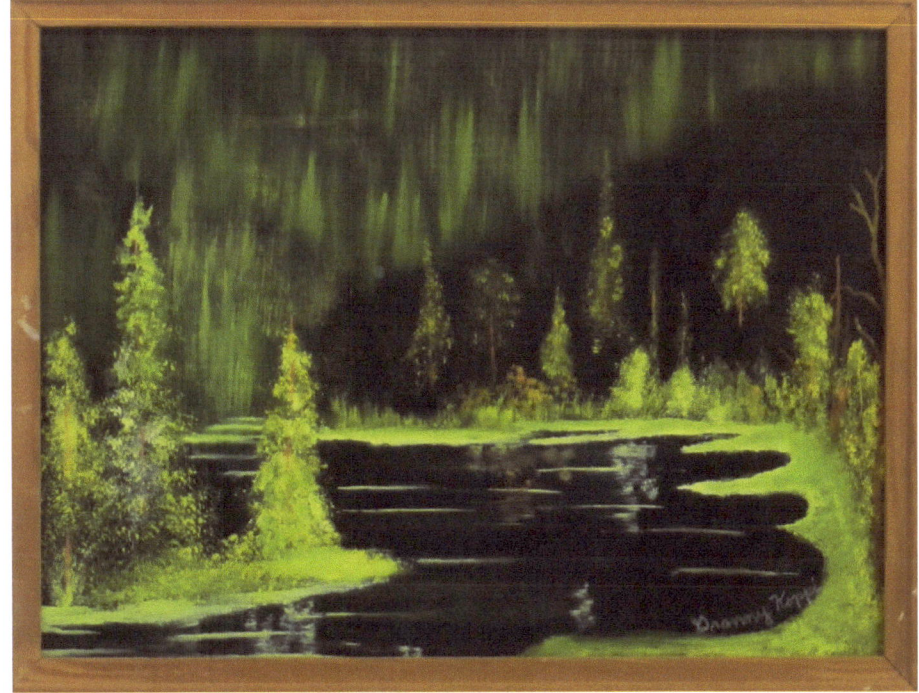

"Radiation Lake"
Granny Koppi, 1980
Melted Apple Jolly Ranchers on asphalt roofing paper

Mary L. Koppi, aka Granny Koppi lived to be 95 and had been an art teacher at the Job Core Center on the side of Mt Hood, Oregon. This plein air landscape was painted at 2 am on a moonless night. She said she was delighted because "It was almost as bright as day and the apple Jolly Ranchers were just the right acid green for the trees!" She believed that painting this radioactive tar lake and drinking a pint of its elixir once a week was the secret to her longevity. At the time of her death Granny's corpse had a radioactive decay half-life estimated at 10,000 years.

K.L.

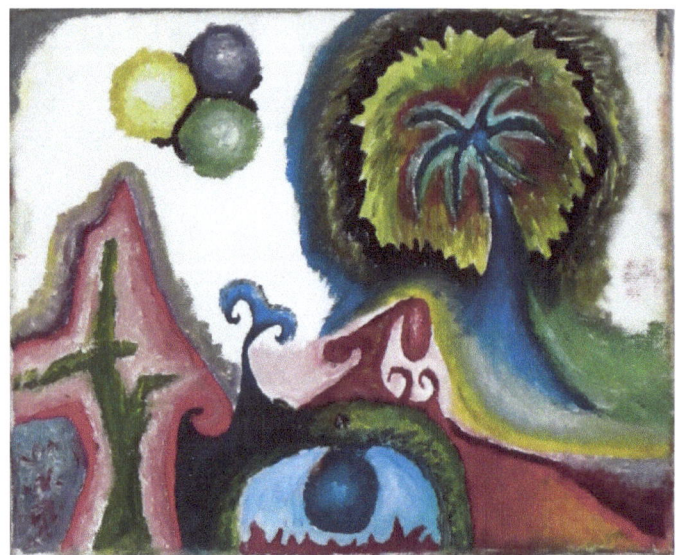

"Recovered From Trash"
Some directionless high school stoner student, 2010
Acrylic and drool on canvas

Homework - smoked a joint
Found some paint and messed around
Wait! … Was that my phone?

K.L.

"Bottoming Out"
Arius Corundum, 1996
Some kind of brown filth, possibly human blood, yellow stain that smells like mustard on canvas

We enjoy artistic challenges, but Corundum has buried the meaning of this painting so deeply that it cannot be exhumed even if we were using a high-speed tractor backhoe. Still, we are intrigued by the Sam Spade detective frisket and he is definitely clutching a Big Mac so it seems logical we may be viewing an emotional miasma, the result of a glycemic crash. We also like the red splatters – because they imply that the artist may have shed his blood for his art, thus appealing viscerally to bloodthirsty viewers and automatically increasing the value of the painting! We are currently awaiting results of the Kastle-Meyer blood analysis.

K.L.

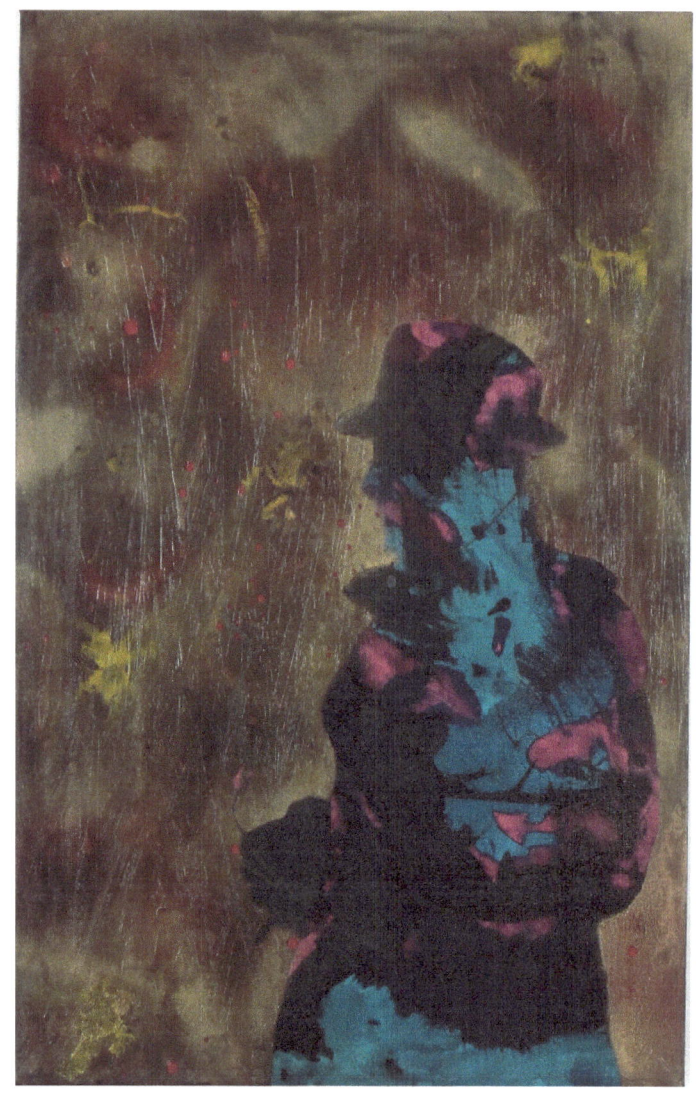

50

"What It Is"
Nate Pocatello, 2010
Acrylic on canvas

It is hello. It is good-bye. It is inhale. It is exhale. It is time to think. It is "so, do you come here often?" It is after sex. It is first thing in the morning. It is the last thing at night. It is tastes good with coffee. It is tastes good by itself. It is the farmers' livelihood. It is an industry. It is something to share with others. It is making new friends 25' from the bar's entrance. It is lung death. It is heart disease. It is yellow teeth and stinky clothes. It is craving. It is late night trips to the store in the rain. It is everything. It is nothing really. It is phlegm in the morning. It is phlegm all the time. It is wheel chairs and air tanks. It is your choice.

K.L.

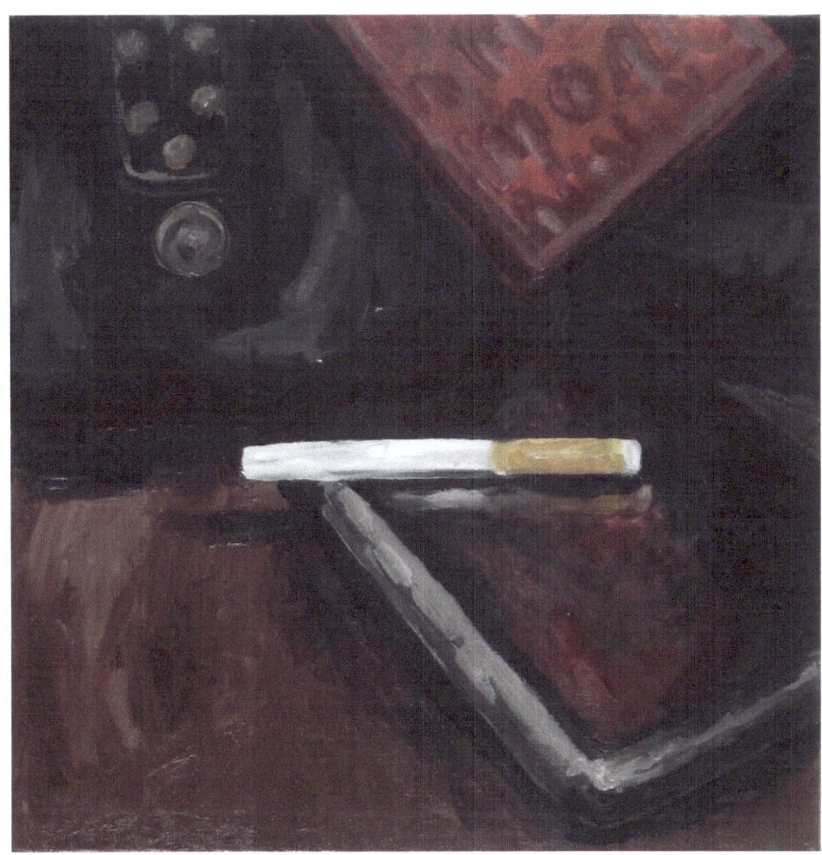

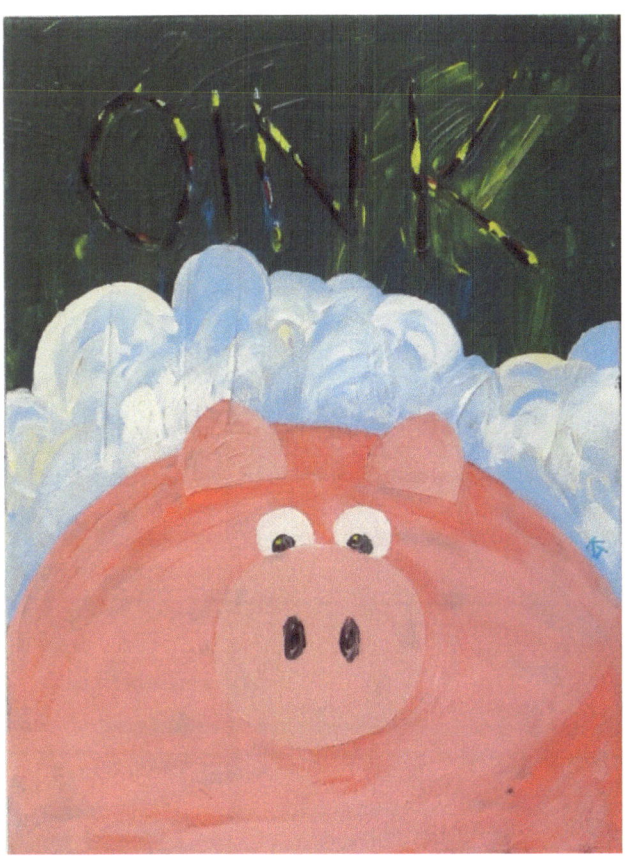

"Wilbur's Getaway"
KT, 1988
Glue, paper-mâché, and melted pink peeps on pigskin

Did you ever wonder what happened to Wilbur after the story was written? Witness a pig's soul ascending, his face illuminated with the joy of having escaped his hell on earth existence on a North Carolina factory farm. The budding artist and ex factory owner, KT, shares his own moment of epiphany with us in a compassionate portrait of Wilbur just moments after the slaughter. KT now travels extensively promoting vegetarianism and soy based bacon. "You know," he says wistfully, "nothing ever went to waste. We used everything but the squeal. But on the other hand, if Saint Peter is a hog, I'm screwed!"

K.L.

"Fun in the Sun"
Barbie Bimboombaugh, 1964
Oil on canvas

It's French Peasant Dress Up Day at Club Rickets and Chloe and Jules are totally down for it. Glancing coyly away Chloe brazenly bares her poor misshapen legs, as her micro cephalic face blushes beneath a fetching apple basket bonnet. Jules' admiring gaze falls upon her loveliness and his skintight bicycle shorts reveal that he is ready for anything because "what you do at Club Rickets, stays at Club Rickets."

K.L.

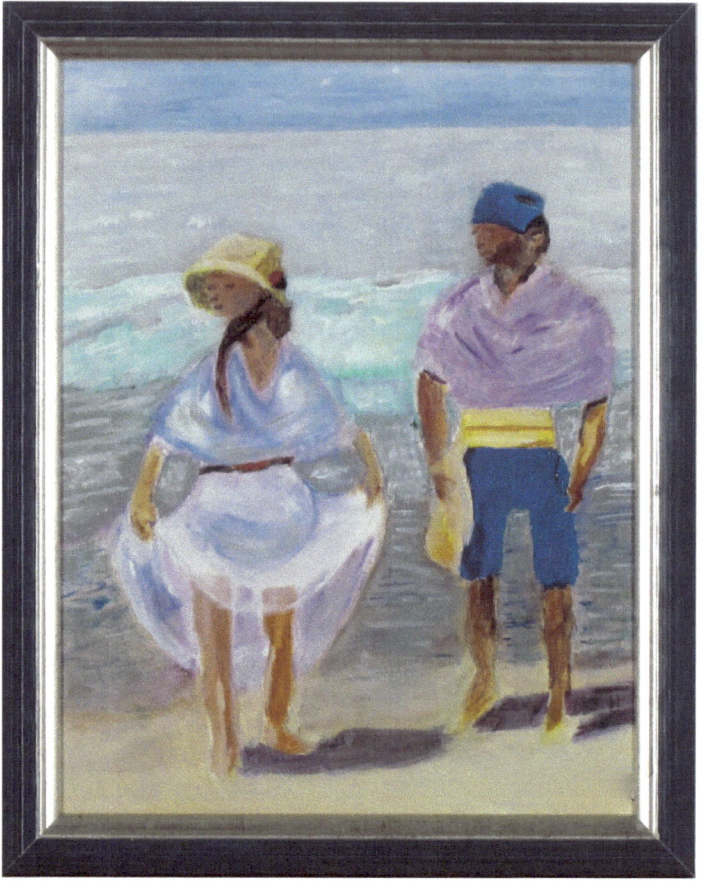

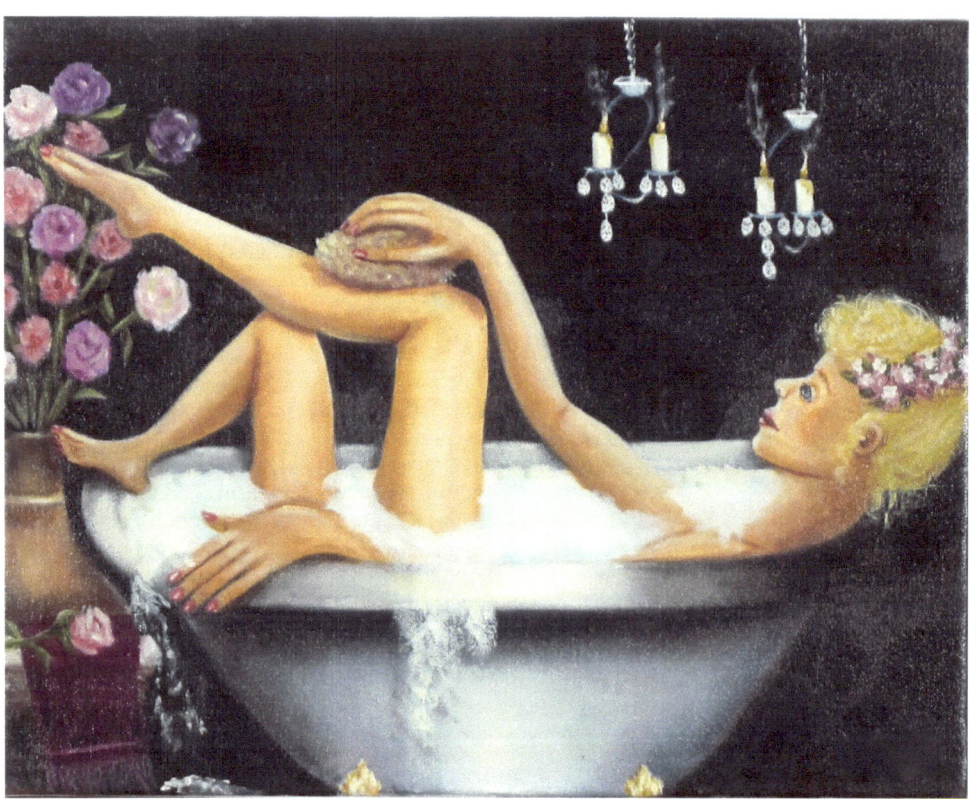

"Polyester Cream"
Pixie Craven, 2011
Acrylic on canvas

Romance, meditation, and cleanliness - confined only by the edges of the canvas, the artist Craven delicately explores the hidden plight of deformed women who bathe in absurdly small tubs of polyester fluff and whip cream. The grisly use of a human brain as a bath sponge is surely a cry for help.

G.O.

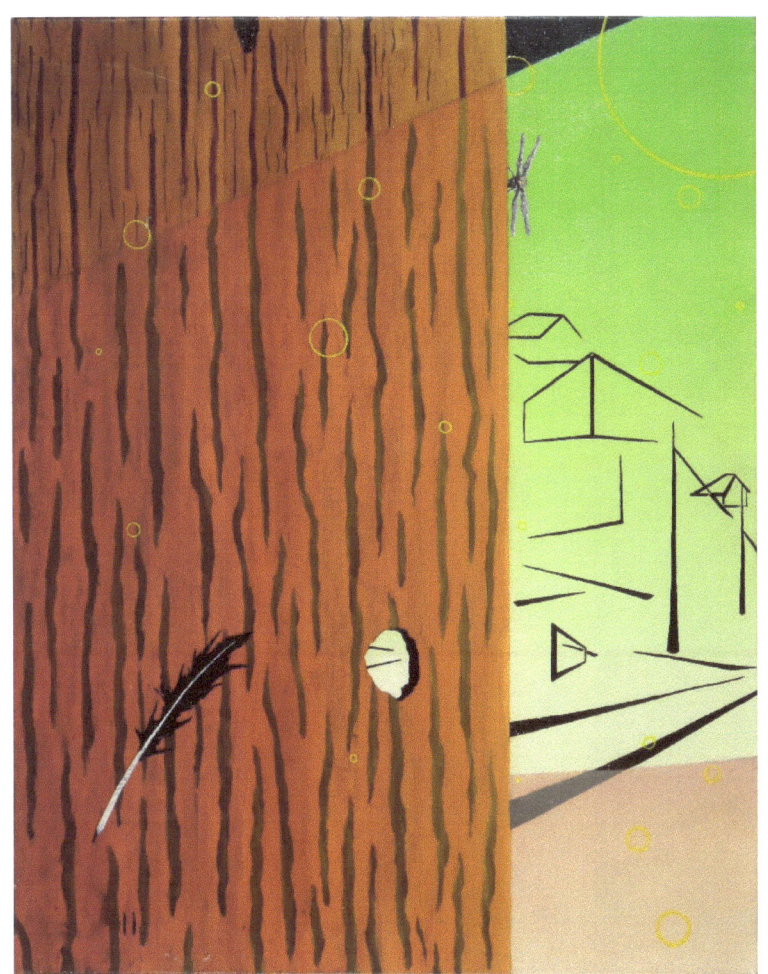

"Dragonfly Watching"
Whistle Britches Riqter, 2011
Oil on canvas

We have it on good authority that this abstract piece represents a peephole view of 200 years hence. It is an angst filled cautionary tale and Riqter's passion guides his brush to give the viewer a bit of a shake up. As a vigorous reference to climate change and rising sea levels, the artist has flooded the lower right with pink lemonade. The tattered crow feather drifts forlornly, suggesting that all non-human animal life is extinct while the champagne bubbles symbolize incessant partying in the midst of doom - denial as it were. The buildings, né civilization, are coming undone, drifting unmoored in a world where gravity is nonexistent. The artist as dragonfly observes from its perch, lost in dragonfly thoughts because, red or blue, that's what they do.

K.L.

"Red Hen With Wagon"
Grandma B, 1986
Oil on canvas

The aging artist Grandma B asks us to make an honest appraisal of ourselves as we look at her work. Are we like the red hen dutifully dragging her burdensome wagon behind her for the length of her days? Unquestioningly she accepts her destiny because she is a ground scratching birdbrain chicken, prone to poopy butt syndrome. Grandma B challenges us to have courage and chart a different course than the bird. But, do we care enough to try? Why should we - when we know most of us will end up in a rest home in diapers with our very own poopy butt.

K.L.

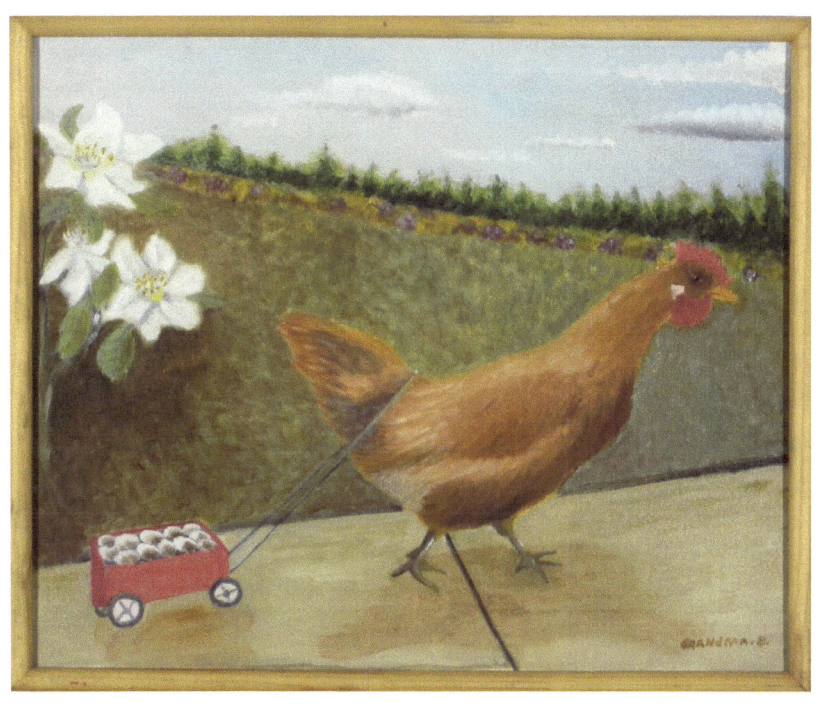

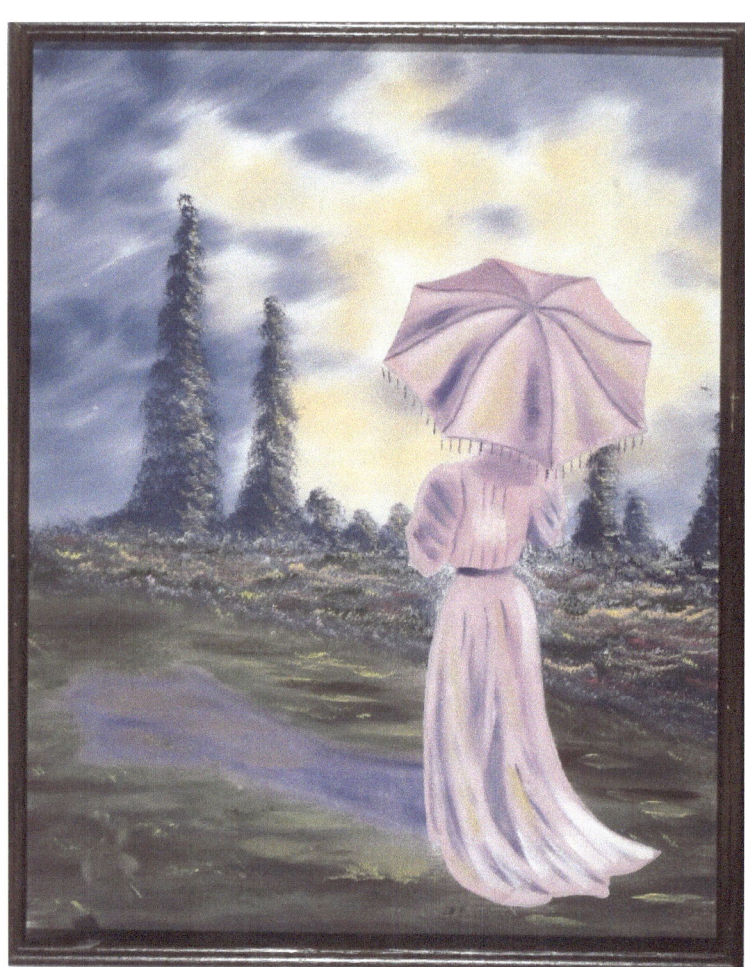

"Sloppy Rich Woman Drags Beautiful Dress in Mud"
Cindie Jensen-Shankelstein, 2012
Acrylic on canvas

Once upon a time Edith Wharton married Bob Ross and begat a sappy pap offspring glowing with violet schmaltz and saccharine romanticism.

K.L.

"Life is short, the art long."
- Hippocrates

"Bride of Frankenstein's Dance Academy"
Septimus Victorious, 1968
Oil on canvas board

It's a classy place – witness the crystal chandelier illuminating the stalactites/chopped cabbage hanging from the cave ceiling. Not just anyone can take dance lessons here. Standards are high and one applicant has been banished into the red desert where she has been reduced to a pillar of salt. The "bride" assertively elbows her way onto the floor as the graceful dancer on the powder blue half shell beams with joyful abandonment. They are unaware of the massive spider approaching to inject his liquefying venom before hoovering their guts out.

K.L.

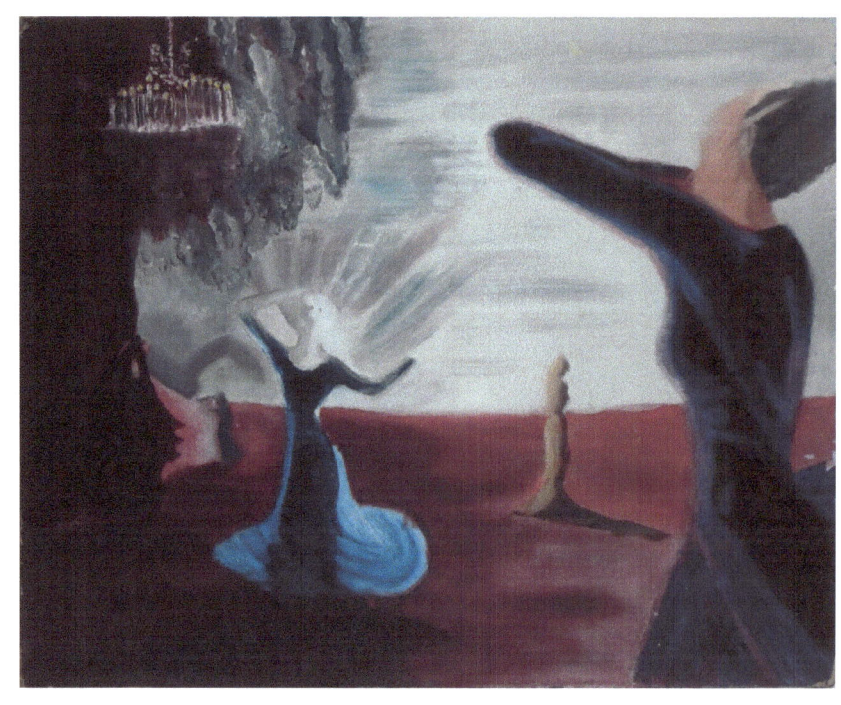

"Redful Relax"
Yaloosey Warmutt, 1950
Acrylic paint and a spoon shaped object on canvas

This seminal work by the American abstract expressionist Warmutt rocked the American West Coast art world upon its initial unveiling at the Modesto Salon of 1950. It is believed that the innovative application of gooey cadmium red paint combined with the use of interpretive earphones produces an alpha meditative state in mesmerized viewers. These people, known as "art zombies", can be seen wherever this painting is shown. In a zoned out state of confused numbness they refuse to go home, but instead pile up in the gallery ignoring the grouchy guards and creating monumental traffic flow problems. This phenomenon was finally solved by installing trap doors in the floor, which dumped hundreds of stunned patrons onto mattresses in the museum basement. Art curators the world over agree that this one painting alone has revolutionized the way museums handle crowd control.

K.L.

"Sun Rings in Ordino Valley"
Slarty Van Codrington, 1957
Acrylic on canvas

The artist grew up in Amsterdam and moved to Andorra in his early 20's. Here, according to the local postman who regularly made the trek to his hilltop aerie with vital supplies, Van Codrington would paint whilst in the grip of powerful hallucinogens. During their frequent sangria evenings, he explained his creative process. After a debilitating stroke, he would grip the brushes in his teeth - hence the anarchic sky that is repeated many times to great effect; the use of his right hand would be reserved for finer work. Urging his children never to start the day with a curse, the smiley-faced moon is indicative of his unbridled optimism, while the dashes surrounding the stars are a nod to an infatuation with mathematics and the Fibonacci sequence. "Sun Rings" was also the name of a recording by the Kronos Quartet commissioned by NASA to incorporate sounds from outer space.

Smedley Codrington

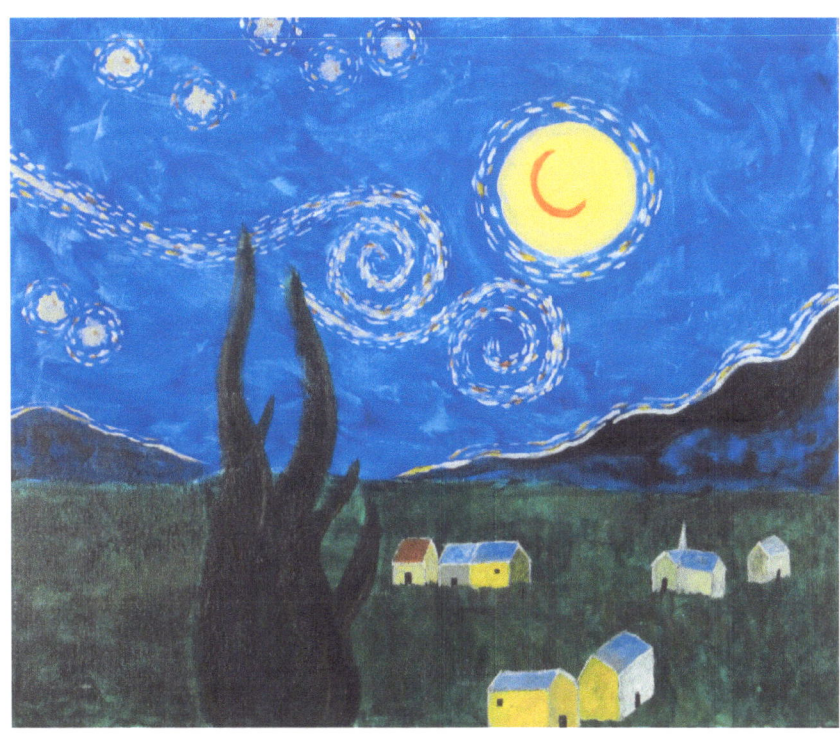

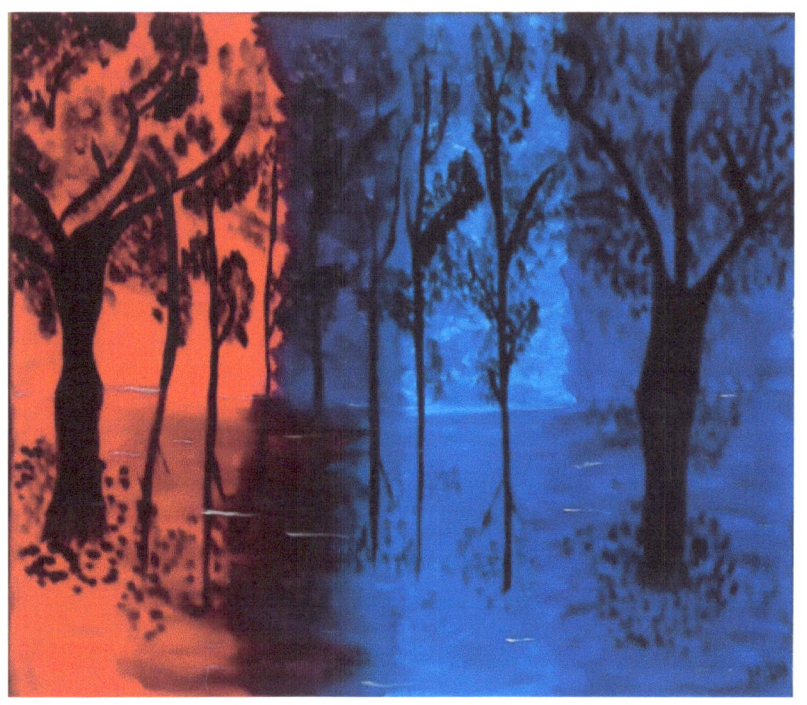

"The Swamps of Polychromatia"
Parson Drexel Weemers aka MW, 1991
Acrylic on canvas

The Dalai Lama once said, "Know the rules well so you can break them effectively." Putting a new spin on this saying the Reverend Weemers appears to be simultaneously learning and breaking them at the same time. His devil may care brushwork driven by a "four colors of the apocalypse" straight from the tube approach draws the viewer into a quiet, dark scene of the artist's making. Are we in a nightmarishly surreal skating rink or a dismal swamp where murder victims have been dumped to feed hungry bottom feeders; either way, this piece is not cheerful. The words creepy and sinister come to mind, also depressing and lonely. Avert your eyes if you do not want to be plagued by nightmares.

K.L.

"Portrait of Silvia"
Artist Unknown, 2013
Oil on board

Hey! Check it out! There was this Halloween party with a "come as your favorite animal" theme. And I decided because I have always, like, had a thing for seagulls, cause they're survivors kinda like me, ya know, that I could, like, be a seagull. But all I could find to use were Thanksgiving turkey feathers. And then when I was hitchhiking to the party in the rain, me and my feathers got soaking wet and they started hanging down, like, all droopy. So when I got to the party I decided to get really fucked up with some of my friends who were drinking "Olde English 800". Then someone pushed me and I face planted in a bowl of cocaine on the coffee table and then like, someone gave me a bottle of tequila and then I don't remember what happened after that. Except that some guy gave me this picture he painted of me which I guess was, like, really nice of him, but I don't think it really looks like me at all.

Silvia Clackstonhughes

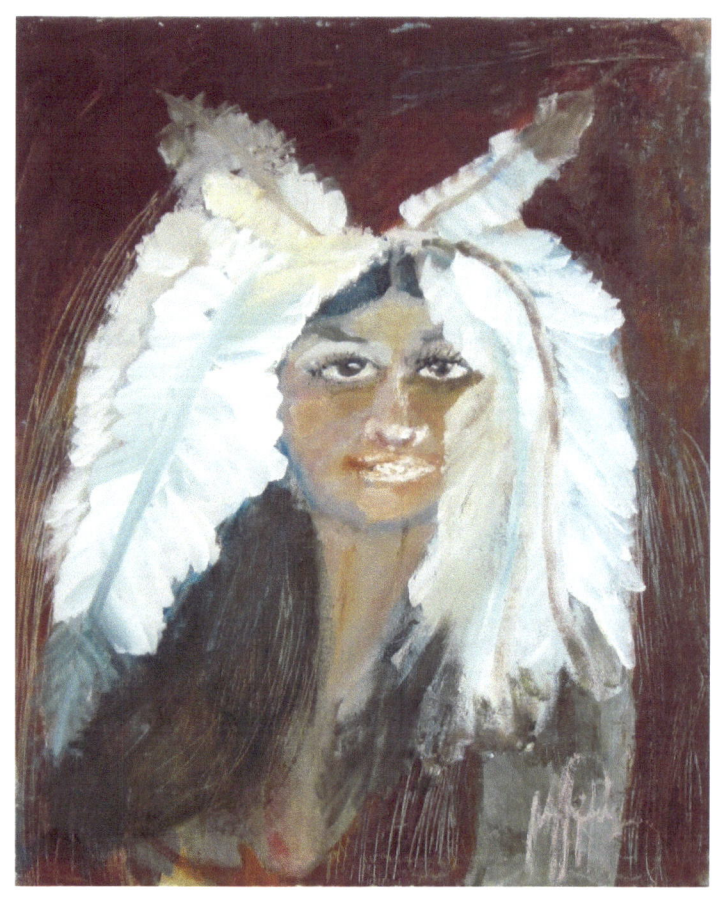

"The Death of Birth"
Edibidac Brown, 1985
Poster paint on cardboard

In this painting the artist's psyche is laid bare for all to
see as he embraces his hidden fears in a highly
symbolic effort that speaks to us about the death of the
American dream: the glowing, relic–like, blue egg
represents society's long cherished, democratic
freedoms, and the deeply buried dagger, oozing blood
from a single wound, represents our species' fatal
shortcomings. The red man, as humanity's collective
higher conscience (some say the artist himself)
reverently kneels, tenderly holding the mortally
wounded noble experiment.

K.L.

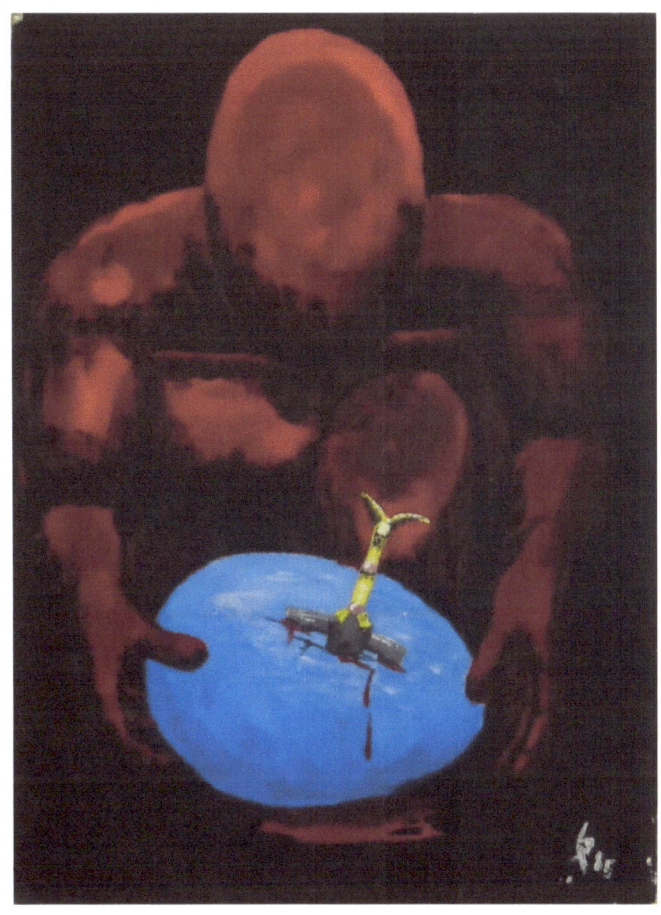

"Mr. Peachly's Precipitous Pique"
Preston Peachly, 1990
Acrylic paint, red chalk on canvas

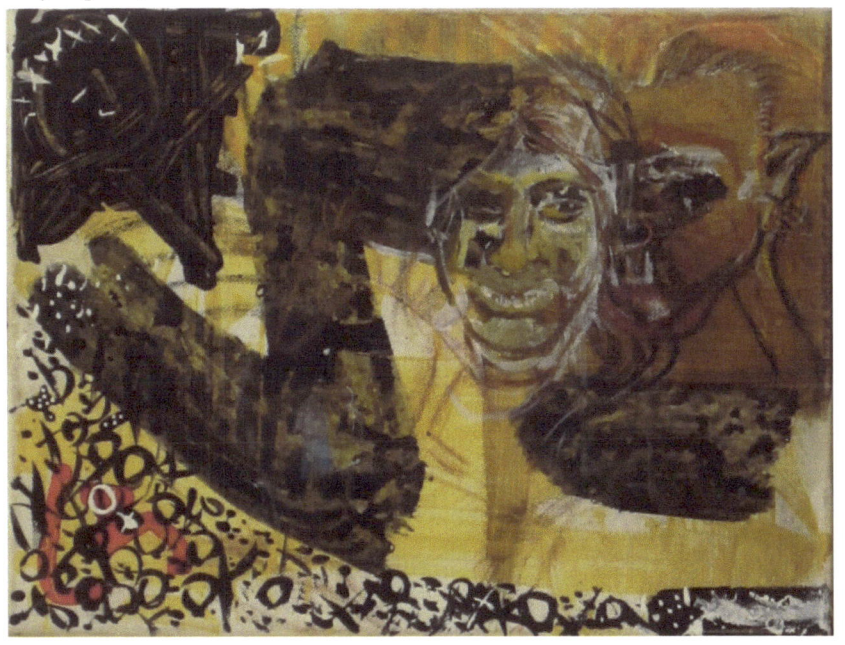

The viewer is introduced to this tangle of self-
portraits by an avalanche of X's and O's
tumbling unexpectedly across the canvas. The
work was likely created as a result of Mr.
Peachly having surrendered his 1997 decade
long national tic-tac-toe championship title. A
sumptuous gold underlayment represents the
millions in lost product endorsements and the
demonic image lurking darkly in the
background may hint at savage revenge. A red
horse, like a ghost from the Lascaux Caves
moves quietly through the jumbled chaos. We
are assailed by a black intestine-like zigzag
writhing dramatically across the canvas just
beneath the finger painted visage of a stoic
Easter Island statue. The wonderfully complex
symbolism and strong emotional content of this
powerful piece hints at, but actually doesn't
even come close to the genius of Francis
Bacon.

K.L.

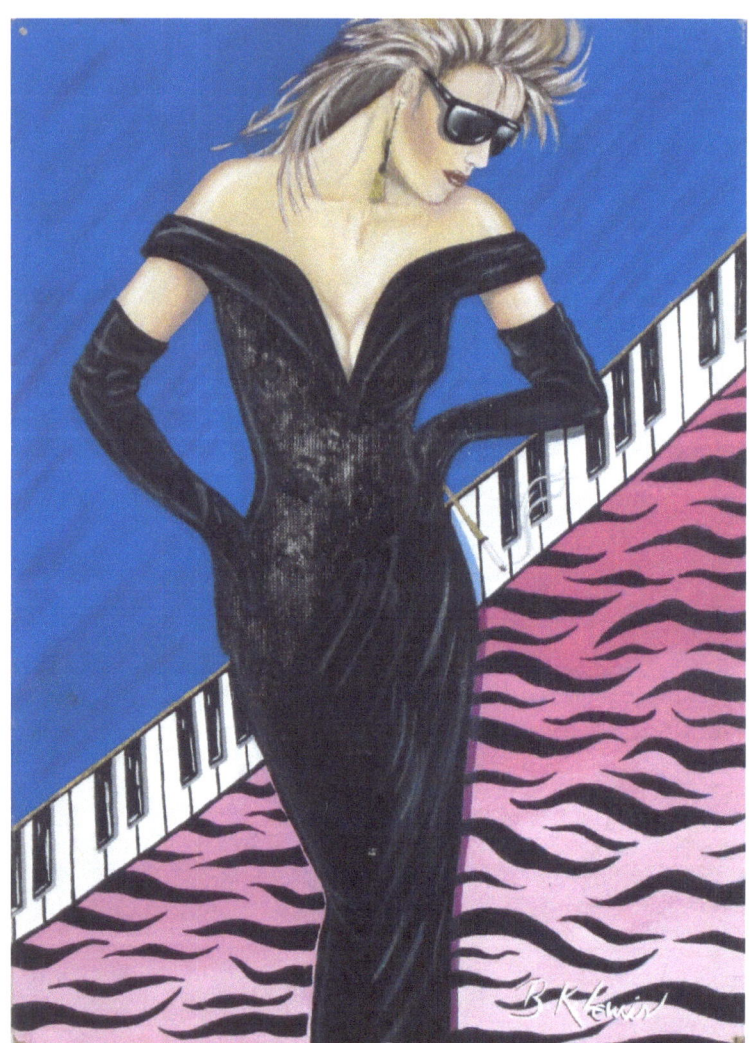

"You Go Girl!"
B.K. Lewis, 1975
Acrylic on canvas board

This striking piece illustrates nothing less than history in the making. Emerging from the screaming, hair pulling hysteria of the Beatles era and the drug addled, venereal disease ridden dens of orgiastic hippy sex, many women were searching for new, liberating pathways to self determination. This swank image of an elegantly attractive performer from the early 1970s glam rock scene epitomized the new role model that many women chose to follow. Inhaling from sophisticated cigarette holders they became fashionably emaciated, and beautifully chic; purple tiger rugs, plunging necklines and push up bras symbolized a brave new direction in their struggle for political and economic equality. Our preeminent social anthropologist consultant, Dr. Anke Steinke, explains that this painting demonstrates the well-known phenomenon of soporific, acquiescent, sheepification (aka SAS) due to a glut of glamorous fashion stimuli upon a repeatedly misled section of the population.

K.L.

"The Cliffs of No Where, No Way"
Dame Dede Smattery, 1986
Acrylic on Masonite board

Subscribing to the theory of, "If I just throw enough paint at the canvas, it's bound to eventually hang together," we see nature here, in shorthand - abbreviated, stylized, simplified, brutalized. What took millions of years to develop is "captured" in an afternoon or possibly a day or two with execrable dry daubs of clumsily layered pigments, vaguely resembling cliffs and trees and sky; all of this on top of an under drawing whose corpselike rigidity results in yet another gilded turd masquerading as a landscape painting. I guess this means we gave it two thumbs down.

K.L.

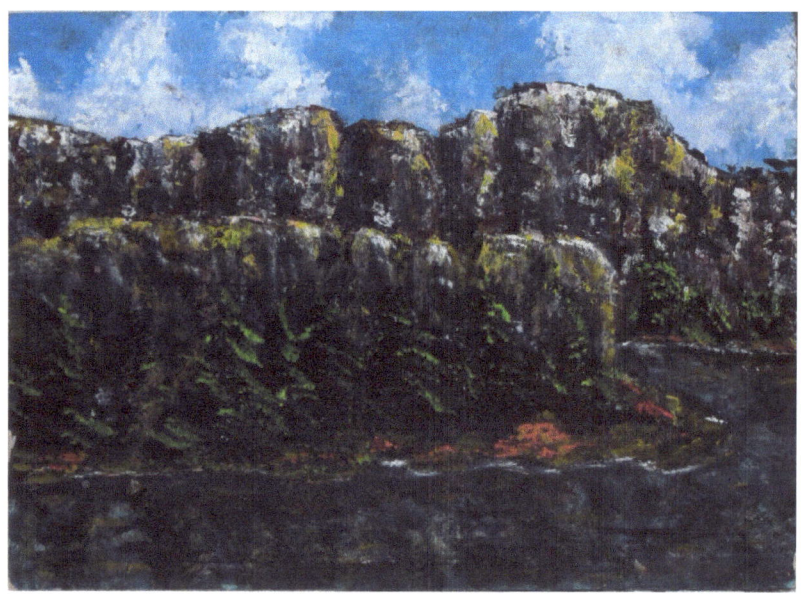

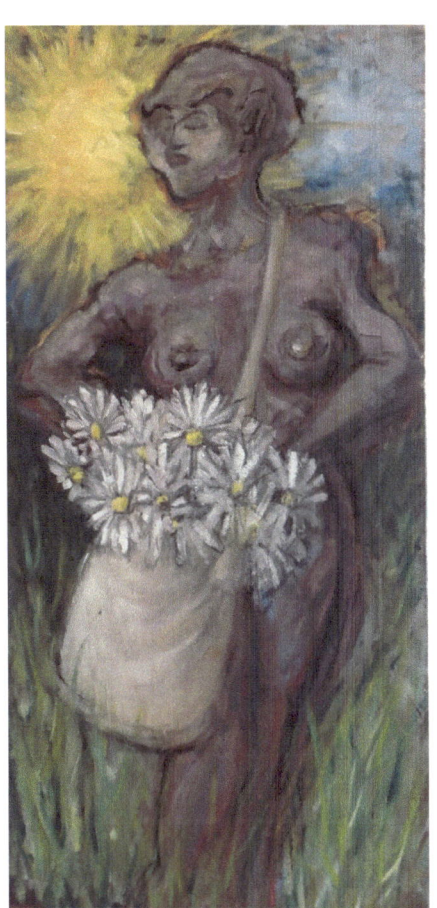

"Big Bosomed Bertha the Daisy Bagger"
Eve DiParadiso, 2002
Oil on canvas

Recovering from a double root canal Bertha spends a day naked in the field picking flowers. A full body second-degree sunburn will take her mind off her jaw pain.

K.L. and J.C.

"There is no logical reason why the camel of great art should pass through the needle of mob intelligence."
– Rebecca West

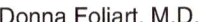

"Armageddon Outta Here"
Donna Foliart, M.D., 1975
Oil on canvas

Forget Mesopotamia – Armageddon is going to be fought on the San Francisco-Oakland Bay Bridge. In this vividly rendered piece, a renowned hospice physician foresees not just the death of her own patients, but the End of the World. On the upper left, fire sweeps down from Heaven, taking out the entire East Bay. Brimstone bubbles over the water as the Beast is about to be tossed from the span whose wobbling cables indicate the intensity of the battle. And on the far right - could that be dust arising from the approach of the Four Horsemen? An inscription on the back of the work explains that the artist, in June 1975, presented this to her father, who then protectively sheltered the work in the back of a dark hall closet for the next 35 years.

Donna Foliart, M.D.

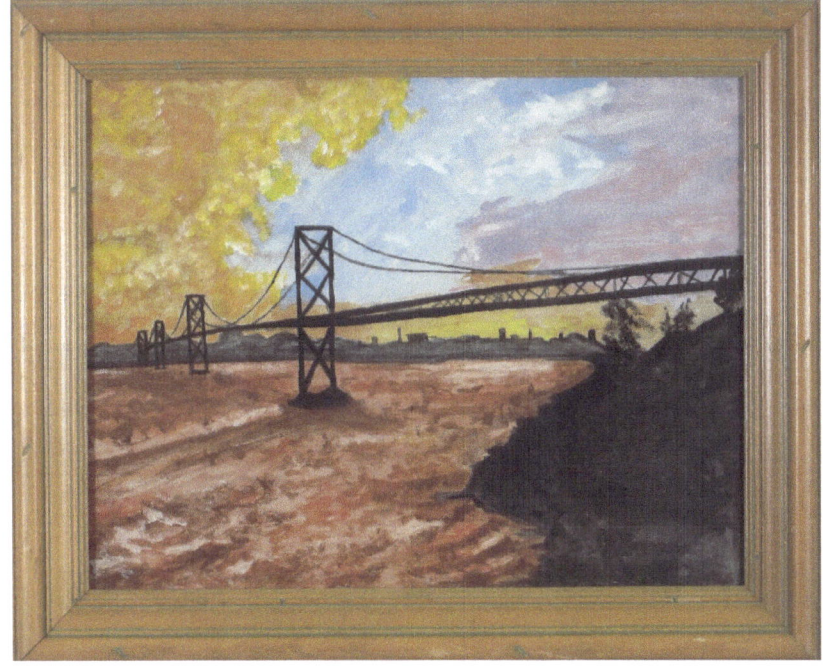

"Becoming Bill, Acid #1"
Timothy Twizzman, 1966
Rare palanquin gutta percha, aged Humboldt County hemp oil, bat feces on Masonite board

While introducing Joan Baez, the great impresario Bill Graham realizes his right hand has morphed into a German Shepherd paw and his nostril is now big enough to shelter a small Shetland pony.

K.L.

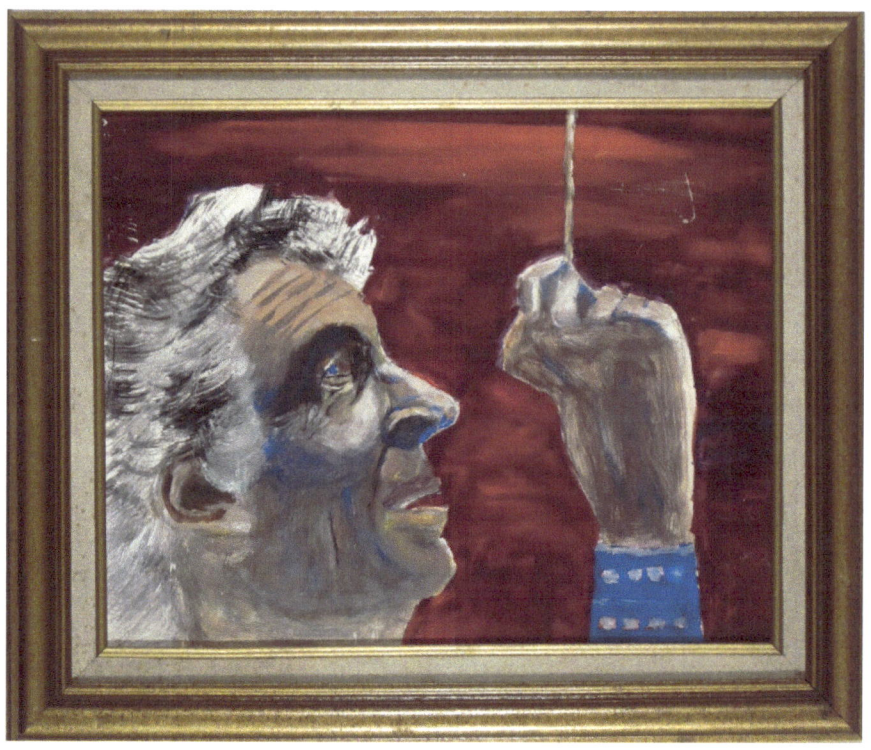

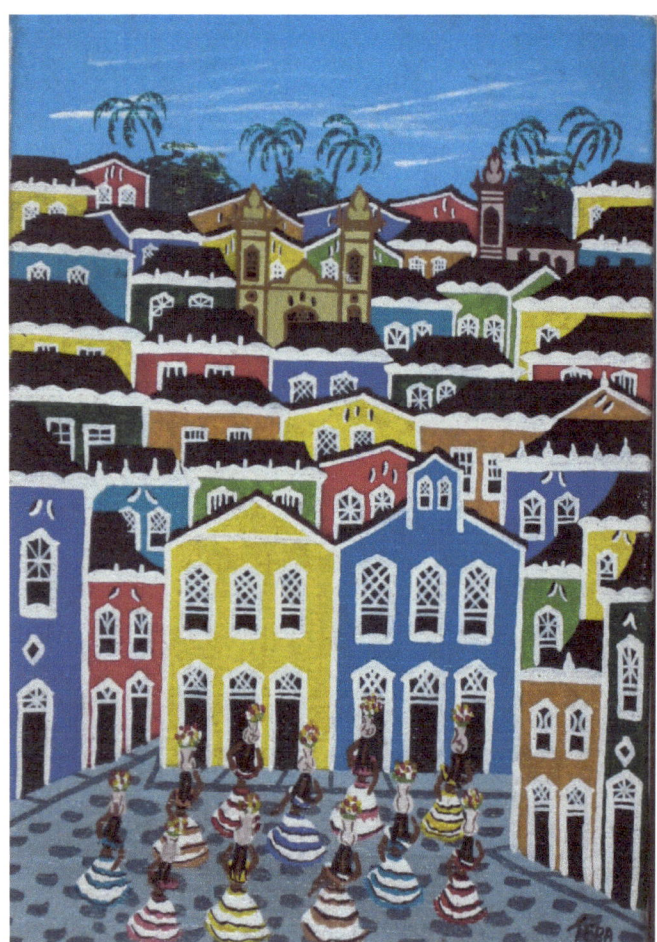

"In the Zone"
Teba Teebers, 1998
Dyed mango sauce on woven corn husks

In a time and place far away where palm trees sway against a light filled azure sky, tiny Carmen Mirandas twirl endlessly in quaintly cobbled plazas and the air is filled with the smell of roasting corn and Mariachi music. Cheerfully colored houses rise up behind them like stacked, 2 dimensional playing cards. Rod Serling appears offering you a long ruffled skirt and a pot of flowers for your head. Bidding you to put them on, he tells you that you will be staying for a while and that he hopes you like dancing…

K.L.

"Sparkling Jubilee"
Little Bill Johnson, her manager, 2001
Oil on canvas

With a malevolent gaze she
calculates her next move. The rubber
glove portends something messy.

K.L.

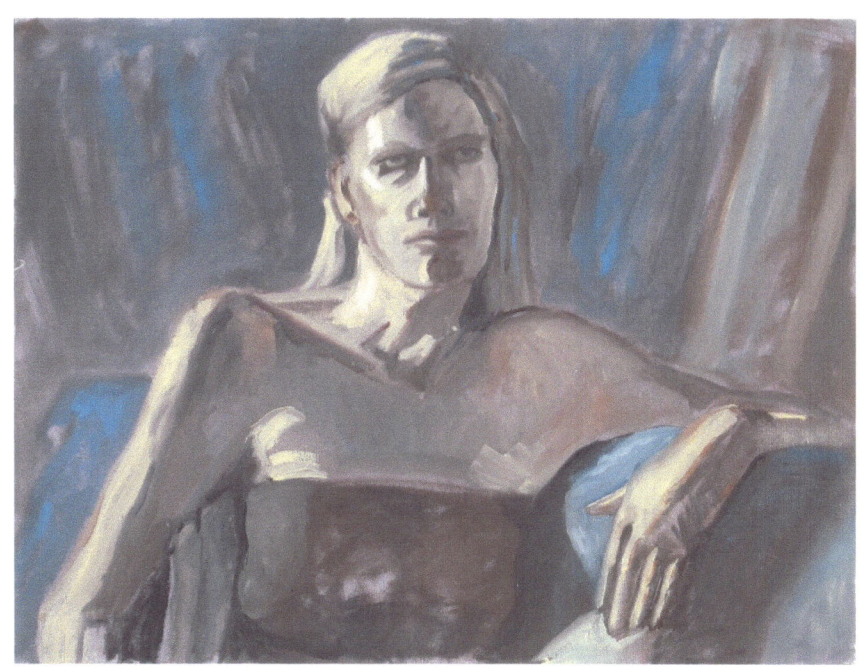

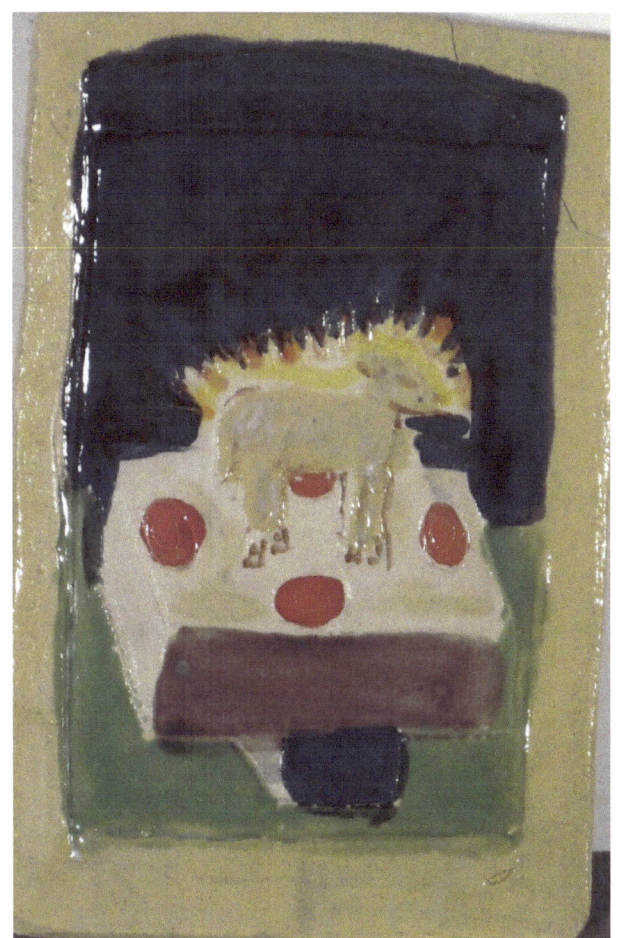

*"Why is art beautiful? Because it's useless.
Why is life ugly? Because it's all ends and
purposes and intentions."*
- Fernando Pessoa

"Hefty Table Holds a Holy Heifer"
Wendell Olafson, 2001
Ceramic plaque

Saint Bessie the barnyard bovine bravely storms the farm
kitchen and climbs onto the dinner table. She is offered fresh
alfalfa and then lead away to be milked, but not until after she
has made an impassioned, barely intelligible speech demanding
the return of Barnie the bull to the pasture and the planetary
benefits of a vegetarian lifestyle.

K.L.

"Holding Up the Sky"
Sri Bubbba Longjohn, 1960
Acrylic on unstretched canvas

Created by the innovative yoga master/artist, Sri Bubba Longjohn, this work illustrates his unconventional approach to combining couples calisthenics with yoga. The symmetrical stability of the work, the wide-open pure blue sky and putting green lawn create an air of tranquility. This piece was one of 12 that graced the reception area of the master's yoga school for decades. It now serves as a cheery bedspread in MCBAG's guest bedroom.

K.L.

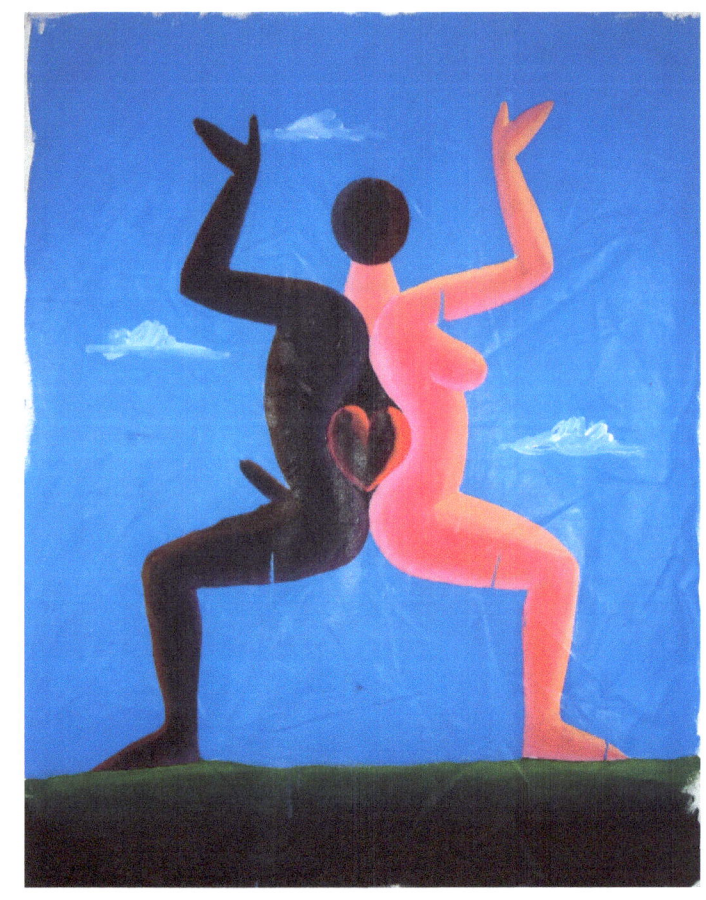

"All art is at once surface and symbol. Those who go beneath the surface do so at their peril."
- Oscar Wilde

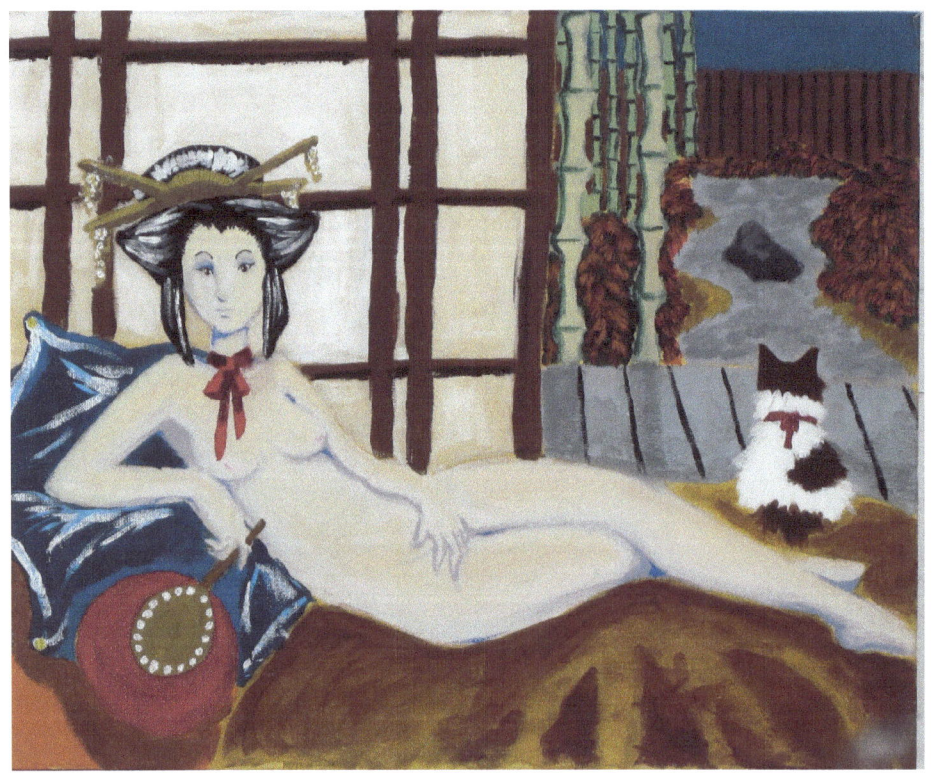

"Two Pussies on the Bed"
Buffy Hamerton, 2000
Acrylic on canvas

Give up, give in, roll over, and perform!
She says yes, I will! Of course I do!
The kitty says no I don't. I won't. Would you?

K.L.

"The Wages of Sin"
Emm Fe, 1990
Acrylic and black sharpie on canvas

Every art collection needs at least one good seduction, addiction, and death piece - and we have found an outstanding one here. Intent on saving our soul, the artist Emm Fe has attacked the canvas with such fervor that she leaves not one bit of space without a paranoid neurotic scribble. The message: Beware of Las Vegas, where you will be set upon by tequila swilling skeletons, flipped off by half naked buxom showgirls, and tempted to stuff your mouth with psychedelic mushrooms - all of this while lovingly holding a razor sharp snickersnee in one hand and an erect microphone in the other. And...oh yes, watch out for the giant pythons that swarm the streets of that wicked town just waiting to finish the job if the booze, babes and drugs don't get you first.

K.L.

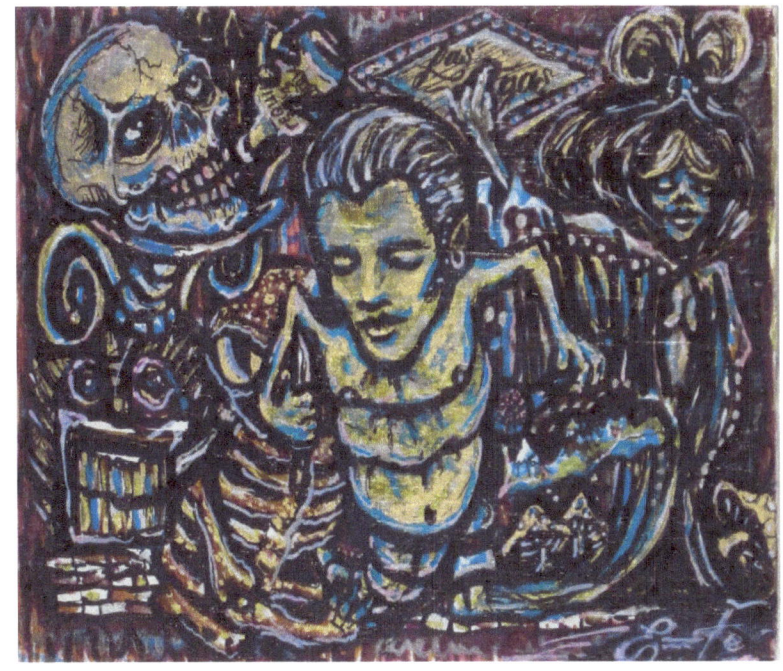

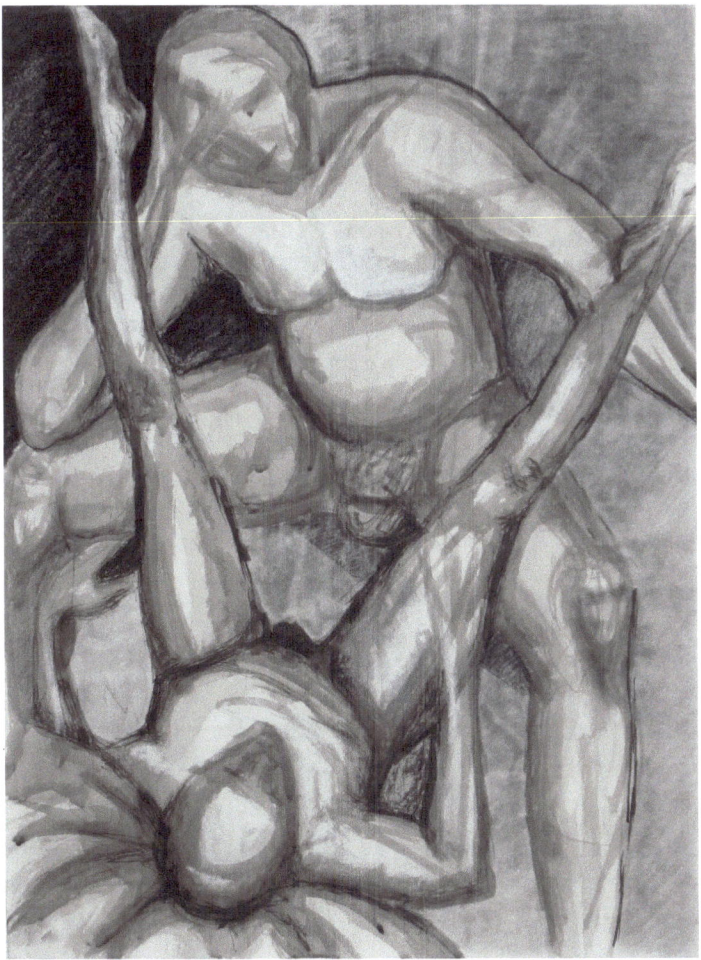

"Life beats down and crushes the soul and art reminds you that you have one."
- Stella Adler

"Don't Leave Home Without It"
Ignatz Astrolux, 2001
India ink, charcoal on shitty cheap paper

John realized, too late, that he had left his junk back at his apartment.

K.L.

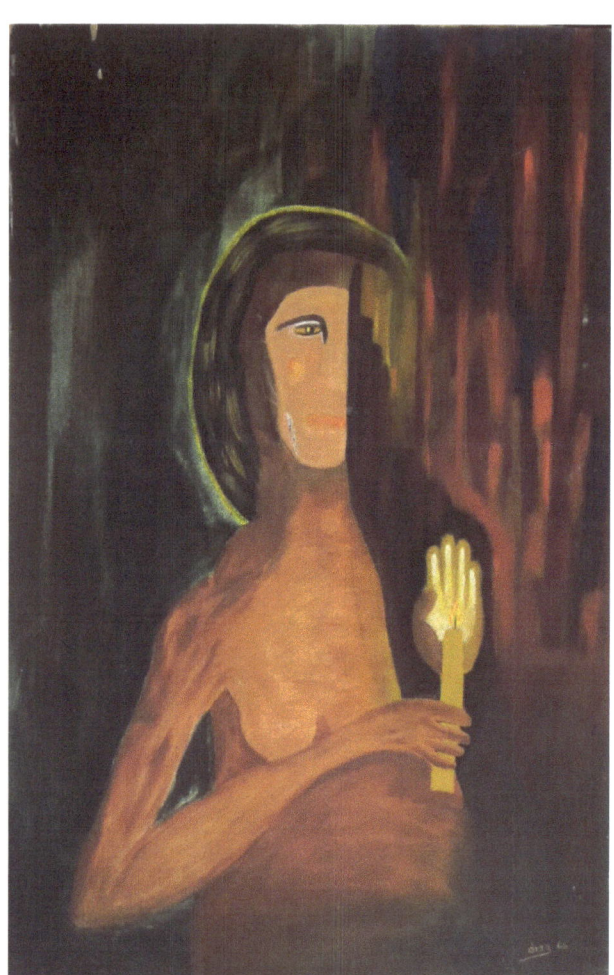

"The Groupie"
Nimrod Diaz, 1966
Oil on canvas

Looking sadly tense, and missing an ear, 9 months pregnant Mary Magdalene stumbles to the outhouse for the 4th time that night. What a fool she was to believe his lines about being the "Son of God" and "I'll save you a place in heaven, baby, right next to me." I mean, Jesus! Any girl would have spread 'em for the Son of God! He had promised her a part in the big story that his friends were going to write about him. He said it would be a best seller for hundreds of years with a shit ton of residuals and that she would be the subject of famous paintings, and something called "movies" many years in the future. Now he's gone and she is left with a big belly, an annoying light behind her head, and a scar on her jaw where some self-righteous bastards at the market place tried to stone her.

K.L.

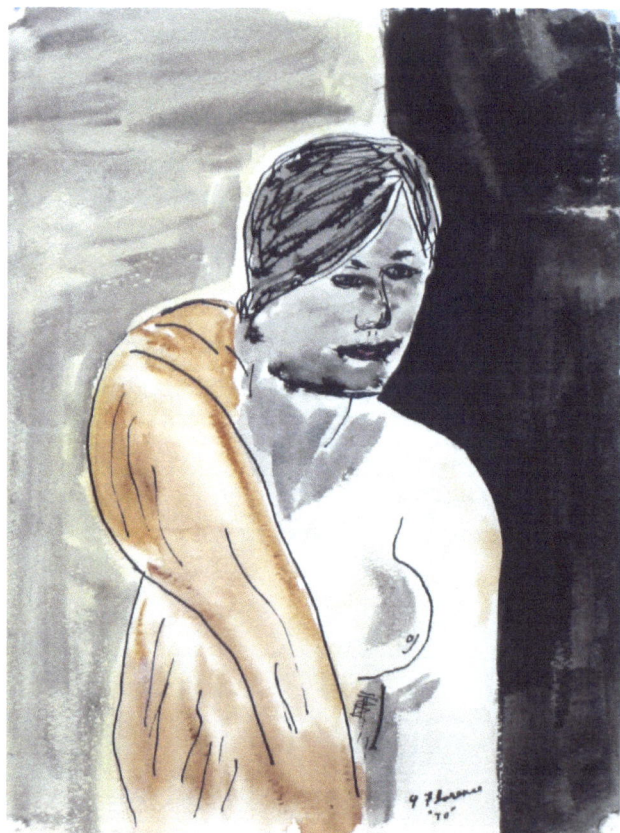

"When Speeches Aren't Enough"
9 Florence, 1970
Watercolor on paper

Who is she and where is she going with the giant over stuffed sausage casing draped like a meat shawl over her shoulder? She is none other than the famous 1970's butchers' union organizer, Maria Macellaio, on her way to a labor rally where she will give one of her famous speeches entitled "The Joys of Nude Chicken Chopping" or "How to Avoid Freezer Burn in the Meat Locker". Typically packing them in, she undoubtedly will have no trouble getting the union brothers' attention with her Mona Lisa smile and focused charismatic gaze.

K.L.

"Nimrod Gets His Rock Off"
Nimrod Diaz, 1970
Oil on canvas

For generations artists have been painting
their dreams as a means to explore the
mindscape of their psyche. In this painting
a vulnerable Diaz portrays himself with a
confused mish mash of feelings. On one
hand looking like a defender of ancient
Troy, he is clearly a superior specimen of
naked masculinity. On the other hand he is
a heavily pelted, lice ridden fellow with a
severely deformed left forearm and no
genitals or sandals. Alone, he sweats and
frowns in the blazing sun, neither building
nor dismantling the wall, but locked forever
in a rigid stance of his own making.

K.L.

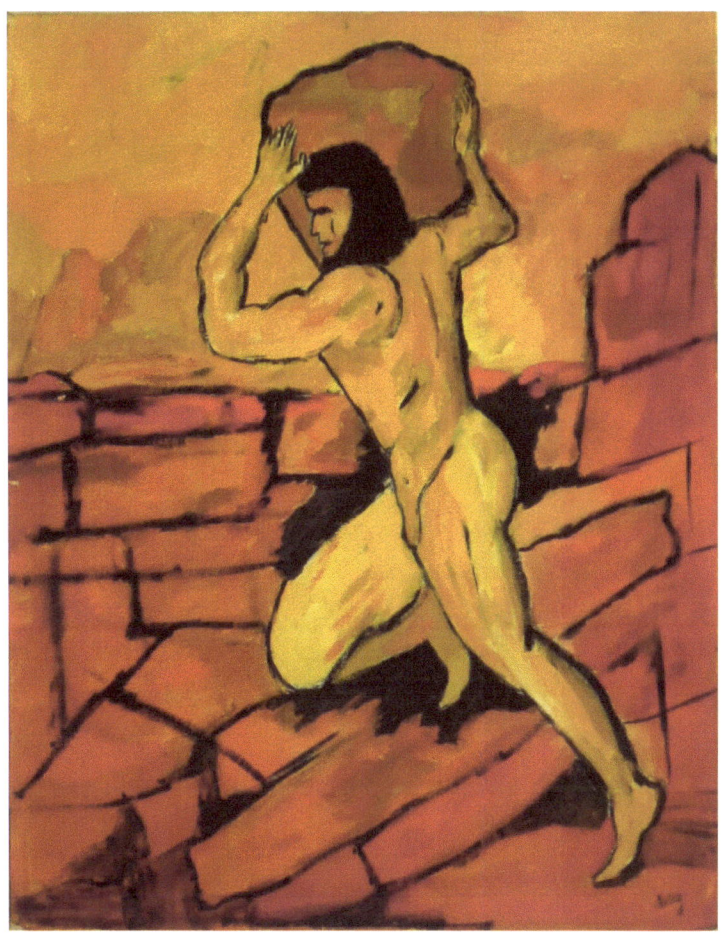

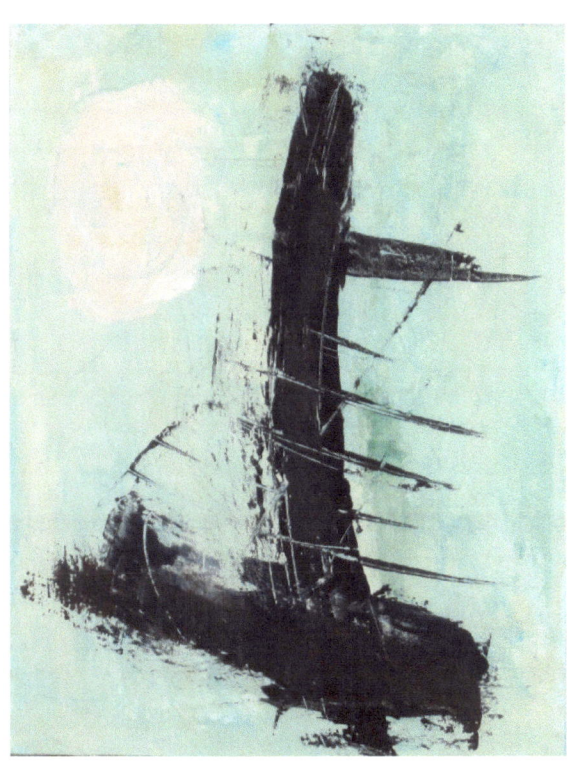

"Getting Really High"
Rudy Maxa, 1985
Oil on canvas

Rising from the grave, the boners of the elderly …
Zeus's sexual desires, a 55-gallon drum of lube, a tribe of warrior
women…
Daddy's belt, my inner demons, an M16 assault rifle…
A zesty breakfast burrito, five-dollar foot longs, big enough to
share…
Hot people, Vikings, catapults…
Opposable thumbs, friction, active listening…
A man in yoga pants with a ponytail and feather earrings, just the
tip…
Pretending to care, support structure is needed, the great
depression…

C.A.H.

65

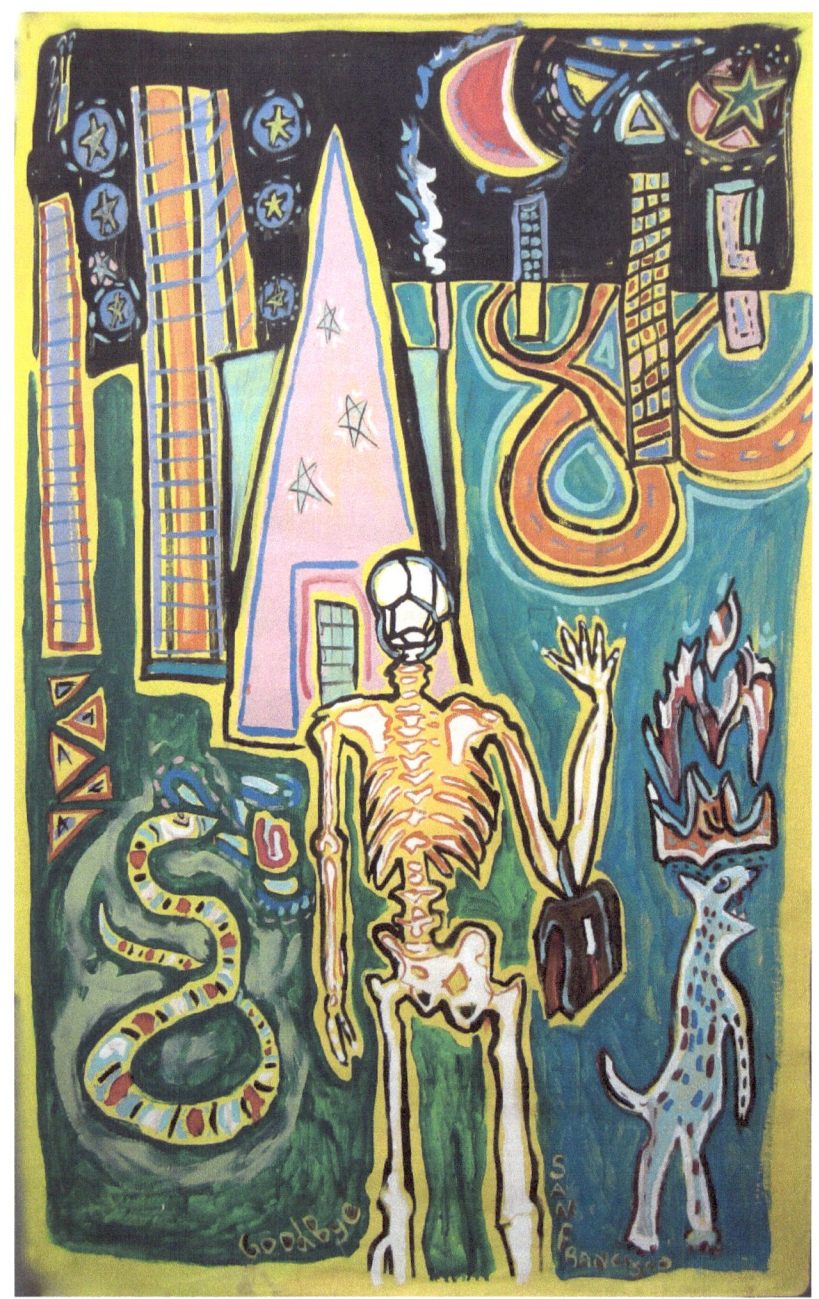

"Goodbye San Francisco"
Bif Dimcheck, 2014
A ground of macerated and boiled Banisteriopsis caapie covered with a light wash of brewed chacruna on Peruvian linen.

For centuries, possibly millennia, artists have been creating while "under the influence". Journey, death, a snake with a beer stein and a dancing cat with a fiery crown – these are strong symbolic indicators of ayahuasca dreaming. Our glowing skeleton friend waves a sad goodbye with its reptilian hand; showing keen fashion awareness, he accessorizes with an expensive leather handbag.

K.L.

66

Acknowledgements

MCBAG would like to thank the following people who have contributed to the creation of this book: Hilary Sheehan, Larry Gilmour, Jeff Carlock, Dan Schiff, Alex Olson, Gabe Olson, Kevin Jones, Francesca Christopher, Donna Foliart M.D., Hugh Visser M.D., Robbie Edwards, Angela Carter, Cards Against Humanity, Diana Lawrence, Kelly Westbrooks, Sally Seymour, and Annie Harte. They all generously contributed wall text and/or art, opinions and advice. It has been most gratifying to have so many fun loving people behind this project.

We would also like to thank Sam Whiting, and Liz Hafalia, staff writer and staff photographer respectively, for the San Francisco Chronicle. They spotted the "brilliance" of this project and gave it its first real public exposure. We also give a shout out to Tiffany Camhi, a most excellent multimedia journalist from Santa Rosa's KRCB radio for interviewing us for that station.

Above all, we want to thank all those courageous artists who may have unknowingly contributed their misshapen, semi-fledged, offspring to this book. We admire their brave efforts and are especially grateful to them. We sincerely hope their creative energies and efforts - in all their forms - continue to spark and burn brightly for all to see, enjoy, and ponder.

"Ah, but a man's reach should exceed his grasp,
Or what's a heaven for?"

- Robert Browning

Marin County Bad Art Gallery MCBAG
Celebrating Creative Failure

Contact us at mcbagcollection@gmail.com
or visit mcbagcollection.com to view our entire collection.

www.ingramcontent.com/pod-product-compliance
Lightning Source LLC
Chambersburg PA
CBHW050748180526
45159CB00003B/1386